Battlegrou

PEGASUS BRIDGE
&
HORSA BRIDGE

British 6th Airborne Division
Landings in Normandy D-Day 6th June 1944

Assault on Pegasus Bridge by Peter Archer

Battleground series:

Battleground Europe

PEGASUS BRIDGE
&
HORSA BRIDGE

British 6th Airborne Division
Landings in Normandy D-Day 6th June 1944

Carl Shilleto

Pen & Sword
MILITARY

This book is dedicated to the memory of all the young men of the 6th Airborne Division who lost their lives in the Normandy Campaign.

On doit des égards aux vivants;
on ne doit aux morts que la vérité.

Voltaire, 1694-1778

First published in Great Britain in 1999
Reprinted 2001, 2004
Reprinted in this version 2010
by
PEN AND SWORD MILITARY
an imprint of
Pen & Sword Books Ltd
47 Church Street
Barnsley
South Yorkshire
S70 2AS

ISBN 978 1 8884 309 7

A CIP catalogue record for this book is available from the British Library.

Typeset in Palatino

Printed and bound in England by
CPI UK

Pen & Sword Books Ltd incorporates the imprints of Pen & Sword Aviation, Pen & Sword Maritime, Pen & Sword Military, Wharncliffe Local History, Pen & Sword Select, Pen & Sword Military Classics and Leo Cooper.

For a complete list of Pen & Sword titles please contact
PEN & SWORD BOOKS LIMITED
47 Church Street, Barnsley, South Yorkshire, S70 2AS, England
E-mail: enquiries@pen-and-sword.co.uk
Website: www.pen-and-sword.co.uk

CONTENTS

CLARENCE HOUSE

This book is dedicated to the men of the 6th Airborne Division who gave their lives in Normandy during the battle for the liberation of France. On 6th June 1944 the role of the Division in the initial assault onto the Normandy coast was to seize, intact, the bridges over the River Orne and Canal de Caen ('Pegasus Bridge') East of Benouville and to establish a bridgehead east of the river to secure these crossings. Additional tasks were to silence the guns of a coastal defence battery south east of Merville and to destroy certain bridges over the rivers Dives and Divette.

These objectives were achieved with great courage and determination. In the early hours of the morning a coup de main party landed in the dark in gliders and captured the bridges, whilst before dawn the Merville Battery had been silenced. The securing of this east flank was vitally important, as it was eventually the hinge on which the entire Allied armies would pivot as they broke out of the bridgehead to sweep on to Paris, Brussels, Antwerp and the Rhine.

Today the Airborne Assault Normandy Trust works to preserve both the memory of those who died in the battle and also the history of the Campaign. As Colonel-in-Chief of the Parachute Regiment, I salute those who took part in the 6th Airborne Division Campaign.

ACKNOWLEDGEMENTS

His Royal Highness The Prince of Wales.

Much has been written about the D-Day landings of the British 6th Airborne Division over the years. This work, originally titled *Pegasus Bridge & Merville Battery*, was the first to be commissioned that extensively guided the battlefield visitor to the exact locations and tells the story, in depth, using the words of so many veterans. Now, the work has been extensively revised and updated and divided into two works; the second titled *Merville Battery & The Dives Bridges*. For this opportunity I would first like to thank the Chief Executive, Charles Hewitt, Editorial Manager, Brigadier Henry Wilson and Series Design Manager, Roni Wilkinson and Jonathan Wilkinson and Jonathan Wright, of Pen & Sword Books Ltd.

My gratitude also to: The Airborne Assault Normandy Trust who have provided me with so much information in the course of my research. My most sincere thanks to the Patron of the Trust, His Royal Highness The Prince of Wales KG KT GCB OM, for his endorsement of my work; also to Lieutenant General Sir Michael Gray KCB OBE DL FI MGT F Inst D, Lieutenant Colonel Joe Poraj-Wilczynski, Major Jack Watson MC and Major Mike McRitchie MC for their support, invaluable assistance and advice with proofs.

I would also like to extend my thanks to the following: Madame Arlette Gondrée-Pritchett of the Café Gondrée and her staff for their wonderful hospitality; and to the Curator of the Musée Mémorial Pegasus Mark Worthington, Director Beatrice Boissee, Assistant Curator Nicolas Dumont and Martin Janssen, Saudrine Gabrol, Pascal Crespin, Rolande Vimond and Halima Fringaut.

The staff at the Commonwealth War Graves Commission

(CWGC) for their tireless work in tending and preserving the war cemeteries in Normandy and for answering all of my numerous enquiries, in particular Barry Murphy, Roy Hemington, Christine Woodhouse, Chris Hawes, Nigel Haines and Peter Francis; Peter Hart at The Imperial War Museum for the use of their sound archives; Eddie Hannath MBE of the Normandy Veterans Association; Beverley H. Davies at The Royal British Legion; and staff at the Public Records Office (now National Archives) in Kew, the Airborne Forces Museum in Aldershot, and the French Tourist Office in London and Caen.

I would also like to acknowledge the overwhelming hospitality and friendship I have received from many of the local people in Normandy who have always made my many visits there all the more worthwhile and enjoyable. Thanks to Delphine Bautmans, Pascaline Dagorn, Patrick Elie, Corinne Hamon (née Lecourt), Marc Jacquinot, Christian Keller, Patrig Lagadu, Lionel Laplaise, Daniela Lemerre, Gérard Maillard, Patrick Moutafis, William Moutafis and Alan Soreau. Thanks also to the many expatriates who also make my visits all the more welcoming, particularly to fellow battlefield guide and historian Stuart Robertson and his wife Jenny Robertson for their hospitality, friendship and company in the many hours shared walking the battlefields.

For my appeals I would like to thank the staff at Channel 4's Service Pals Teletext Service, Editor John Elliot and Chris Kinsville-Heynes from *Soldier* Magazine, Colonel K. Coates Editor of *The Pegasus Journal*, Robert Beaumont of *The Yorkshire Evening Press* (now *The Press*) and Mike Laycock, also thanks to the secretaries of several regimental associations and Ken Wintle for the use of his extensive appeal database.

As always, the most interesting and rewarding part of this type of research is gained through interviews and correspondence with the veterans themselves. To hear their first-hand accounts of the events, and on occasion escort them around the Normandy battlefield; often concluding with a visit to the War Cemetery at Ranville so that they may pay their respects to their fallen comrades, has been, and always will be, a great privilege. Overwhelmed by the response to my appeals, I must apologise to those whose anecdotes I have not been able to use because of the inevitable editorial restrictions.

Thanks to the many veterans and their families who have kindly loaned valuable documents or photographs. A few I would like to mention, who have helped specifically with this work, are: R. Daeche, R. Deller, Peggy and Mary Eckert and family of Cyril and Stan Eckert, Denis Edwards, Major Ellis Dean MBE MC, Ted George, Major John Howard DSO, David 'Dai' King, Bill McConnell, H. Pegg, Edward Pool MC, Brigadier G. Proudman CBE MC, family of John Rollingson, James Sanders, family of Peter Sanderson, Maurice Segal, Ray Shuck and family, Norman Stocker, Ernie Stringer, Richard Todd, Major N. Ward, Major Jack Watson MC, Harry White and family of George White, Charlie Willbourne and Major Anthony Windrum.

Thanks also to Don Mason, who passed away before the completion of my manuscript for the first edition of this work 1999, and I offer my condolences to his family. Sadly, many other veterans, some who became very close friends, mentioned in this acknowledgement have also passed away in the time leading up to this extensively revised and updated new edition. While their company and presence is sorely missed, their memory lives on as strong as ever. I hope this work helps to preserve some of that memory for posterity.

Others who have assisted or provided valuable information are Revd. Neil Allison, David Ashe, Neil Barber, Ted Barwick, Captain R. Clark, Danny Grenno, Lt Cdr W. N. Entwhisle RN, Cheryl Hamilton, Paul Harlow, Helen Hartley, Mark Hickman, Al Jones, Michiels Kris, Tony Lea, Lt Cdr John Lavery RN, William J. Lewis Platt, Major Will Mackinlay, Paul McTiernan, Angus Newbould, Doug Oxspring, Keith Petvin-Scudamore, Paul Reed, Victoria Raynor, Carl Rymen, Paul van Rynen, Chris Summerville, Capt G. M. Timms and Mike Woodcock.

Thanks to Dave Popplewell for sharing his extensive knowledge on German and British vehicles, weapons and unit formations, and for his generous assistance in proof reading and checking of statistics. Thanks to Lance McCoubrey for help with maps and sketches and to the late Lieutenant Colonel Sir James Stormonth Darling CBE MC TD for his advice. Also to my late dear friend military historian, author and former Associate Professor, Charles Whiting; for sharing his unquestionable knowledge of the Second World War and his literary skills. Thanks also to other friends who have been supportive of my work.

Special thanks, and love, go to my family: to my daughters Michaela and Hannah for their interest and curiosity in their father's work. They have both made wonderful travelling companions around the battlefields over the years. Thanks also to them for putting up with a dad whose head seems forever submerged in papers, books or behind a camera lens. Last, but by no means least, to my 'other half', Irena, for her patience, interest, help and hours of tireless proof reading during my research and writing; and without whose constant support and help, I would not be able to complete any of the many projects I undertake.

Any errors in the text are mine alone, and if anyone can provide any further information about, or photographs of, any individuals, veterans or places relating to the 6th Airborne Division in Normandy, please forward any details to **fallenheroes@btinternet.com** Please add '**6 Ab Div**' as the subject title.

To everyone I hope my work justifies all our efforts.

Spring 1944, German coastal troops prepare for the Allied invasion.

INTRODUCTION

It was during the course of my research in Normandy that I became aware of the dedicated efforts of a number of people who have all volunteered their time to uphold the aims set out by a trust that was initially proposed by the Commander of the 6th Airborne Division, General Sir Richard Gale. Supported by General Sir Anthony Farrar-Hockley, then Colonel Commandant The Parachute Regiment, the Airborne Assault Normandy Trust was founded to preserve the history of the 6th Airborne Division's assault into Normandy with the following aims:

* To provide a memorial, in France, of the airborne assault into Normandy in 1944.
* To honour the many who gave their lives in achieving success.
* To preserve the memory of the vital part played by the French people of the region as well as that of the assault force.
* To continue into the future the happy relationships of wartime years between the people of Normandy and the liberating forces.
* To preserve and accurately relate the history of the 6th Airborne Division and other Allied forces which operated in the area in the first few days after 6 June 1944.

There are two main projects that the Airborne Assault Normandy Trust has helped to finance over the years:

The first has been the preservation of *Musée de la Batterie de Merville* (The Merville Battery Museum). Opened in 1982, to date, extensive work has been carried out and it has been transformed into the wonderful museum that you can see today (see *Merville Battery & The Dives Bridges* by Carl Shilleto). It is hoped that one day the whole site will eventually be restored to its original condition complete with rearmament and the opening up of the underground chambers and tunnels.

The second, in conjunction with the *Comité du Débarquement*, is the *Musée Mémorial Pegasus* (Memorial Pegasus Museum). Opened on 4 June 2000, by HRH The Prince of Wales, the memorial park is dedicated to all those who served in Normandy with the British 6th Airborne Division. The centrepiece of the memorial garden is the original, and now restored, Pegasus Bridge. The bridge was relocated, having been rescued from a nearby field where it had been left to rust, after it was replaced in 1994 from its position over the Caen Canal.

Like all registered charities though, despite the tireless efforts of its members, the Trust is reliant upon public donations and in need of more funding if it is able to maintain its aims and turn future project ideas into a reality. If you wish to ensure that this part of our history is to be remembered by future generations, then the Airborne Assault Normandy Trust would be most grateful of any donation, however small, to help them achieve their aims. All donations should be forwarded to: The Airborne Assault Normandy Trust, Regimental Headquarters, The Parachute Regiment, Browning Barracks, Aldershot. Hampshire, GU11 2BU. All donations, made payable to the Trust, will be gratefully acknowledged.

Whatever the contribution, it is a small price to pay for the freedom that we have gained through the sacrifice of so many young men who will never return from the battlefields of France.

Carl Shilleto
RANVILLE, FRANCE

Drilling for the inevitable Allied landings.

ADVICE FOR VISITORS

Your visit, to the 6th Airborne Division area of operations, will cover ground in the north-eastern part of Calvados, which is the smallest of Normandy's five departments. The scene today is one of a picturesque countryside, with half-timbered houses and sprawling farmland reminiscent of what it must have been like before the invasion and inevitable destruction that came in 1944. The towns and villages have long since been rebuilt and have grown in size to accommodate the ever increasing population. New roads now make travelling across the area more comfortable and quicker than anything that was experienced by the troops during the Second World War and the lunar landscape of carpet-bombed countryside has once again returned to smooth, lush, green grazing land or to golden fields of corn. Still clearly visible in places though, are the high hedgerows and small fields that make up the infamous *bocage*.

A visit during the winter months will allow you to see the area in the Dives valley partially flooded, although the floods are never as extensive as they were back in June, 1944. I recommend that the best time to visit the area is during the summer when the climate is more agreeable, places of interest are open and you are seeing the environment in climatic conditions similar to that experienced by the troops during the campaign itself. Normandy is very much like the British climate with unpredictable rainstorms. The only exception is that in summer it is likely to get very warm; therefore sun cream, sunglasses and a bottle of water are all sensible additions to your travelling pack. Also include a small first-aid kit and a comfortable rucksack to carry everything in. Sturdy shoes or walking boots are essential and good waterproofs should also be taken as rain storms can be torrential.

For British Nationals, in case of any accident or illness that may require medical attention, you should take your European Health Insurance Card (EHIC) This is available online via the National Health Service (www.nhsdirect.nhs.uk - type EHIC into the search bar), by telephone 0845 606 2030, or by post (application form available at your local post office). This will cover medical treatment in France. Also ensure that your tetanus jab is up to date and it is advisable to take out medical insurance while travelling abroad.

Emergency numbers in France are: 112 for any emergency service, 17 for the Police, 15 for an Ambulance and 18 for the Fire Brigade. The Operator is 13 and Directory Enquiries is 12. When telephoning the UK dial 0044 then the UK area code minus the first 0, and then the number you require. Finally, do not forget that a valid ten year British passport is still required for British Nationals to enter the country.

A camera, plenty of film or memory cards, and a notebook and pencil (ink smudges when wet) are the best way to record your visit, but don't burden yourself with unnecessary equipment. A tripod is not really essential (unless you are going to be taking photographs in low light or of yourself) and the average compact digital zoom camera will more than meet your needs. For the more avid photographer, I find an SLR and 10-20mm, 18-70mm and 70-300mm lenses are an ideal choice. Remember not to shoot into direct sunlight and a good tip if taking pictures of headstones or memorials is to get down to the same level and, when the light is bright; take your picture from an oblique angle so that the inscription is defined by the shadow.

Unlike the static trench warfare of the First World War, where the fighting was carried out on the same battlefield for several years, the Second World War saw the arrival of modern warfare; here technology played as greater part in the battle, as did the men who had to fight it. However, despite the weapons of mass destruction, the task of securing an area and expanding the bridgehead was still left to the men on the ground, the infantry. Unlike their forefathers though, these men would find themselves making advances over ground in days rather than months and years. Consequently, you are unlikely to find anything in the way of old munitions lying about today on or beside the well-trodden tourist tracks. Nevertheless, there are still many munitions left over from the battles, buried beneath the ground or in woods and pathways off the beaten track. There are also other grim discoveries still being found today.

On 8 May 2009, the bodies of five German soldiers, still wearing their metal identity tags, were found in a shallow unmarked grave near Bavent. The remains were reinterred at the German cemetery at la Cambe. On 14 February 2010, some 20,000 of Caen's 110,000 inhabitants had to be evacuated when a 1,000lb (453kg) Allied bomb was found during building work at Caen University. A bomb disposal squad safely disarmed the bomb. If you do find something unusual, do not touch!

What also remains today are the extensive fortifications that once formed part of Hitler's Atlantic Wall. Positioned all around the Norman countryside these concrete monoliths remain as formidable and awesome as they were over half a century ago. Normandy also has what is probably the greatest concentration of war memorials, than any other battlefield in the world. Over 200 are connected with the 6th Airborne Division alone.

Maps and Satellite Navigation
The most detailed maps of this area are IGN SÉRIE BLEUE (Series Blue). You will need two: the 1612OT 1:25000 CAEN map and the 1612E 1:25000 DIVES-SUR-MER. CABOURG map. The IGN SÉRIE VERTE (Series Green) 1:100 000 No 6 map is also useful if you wish to explore the rest of the Normandy landing beaches or American airborne sector. Maps may be ordered via most good bookshops or online (www.ign.fr).

To assist those who have satellite navigation equipment there is, in Appendix D of this work, a list of the satellite navigation coordinates to all the places of interest and locations of many of the memorials and exhibits that are mentioned in the text. For the armchair tourist and traveller alike, I can recommend using these coordinates to reference places on www.earth.google.com. The resources available on this site, along with the aerial photography, are particularly valuable to the reader as it will allow them to understand the distances involved and appreciate the terrain of the area more easily.

Travel and Accommodation
Travelling to this part of France is probably best done by using one of the ferry companies: Brittany Ferries (www.brittanyferries.com) sailing from Portsmouth to Caen (approx. 6hr day crossing and 7hrs at night), Portsmouth to Cherbourg (high-speed 3hr crossing); LD Lines (www.ldlines.co.uk) sailing from Portsmouth to Le Havre (approx. 5hrs day crossing and 8hrs at night); P&O Ferries (www.poferries.com) from Dover to Calais (approx. 1hr 30mins crossing). The latter will involve a 3 to 4hr drive from Calais to Caen but can work out to be a cost-effective way of travelling, even with the added cost of the toll roads, called the *Péage*. From Calais you take the A16 to Boulogne and Abbeville, the A28 towards Rouen, then the A29 towards Le Havre and finally the A13 to Caen.

If driving, comprehensive insurance is advisable. If it is your own vehicle you must carry the original vehicle registration document (V5), if it is not your vehicle you must have a letter from the registered owner giving you permission to drive. A full valid driving licence and current motor insurance certificate is also required and an international distinguishing sign (GB) should be displayed on the rear of the vehicle (unless your vehicle displays Euro-plates). You should also carry spare bulbs as it is illegal to drive with faulty lights. A high visibility reflective jacket in the passenger compartment, in case you need to exit the vehicle after a breakdown, and a warning triangle to be used in conjunction with the vehicles hazard warning, are also compulsory. Headlight beams should also be adjusted for right-hand driving using headlight convertors.

The minimum age for driving a car is eighteen years. You should not drink alcohol and drive. Seat belts are compulsory for all occupants and children under ten years of age are not permitted to travel in the front of the vehicle. As a general guideline, speed limits (unless otherwise indicated) are: 130kmh (80mph), or 110kmh (68mph) when wet, on motorways (*autoroutes*); 110kmh (68mph), or 100kmh (62mph) when wet, on dual carriageways; 90kmh (55mph), or 80kmh (49mph) when wet on open roads; and 50kmh (31mph) in built-up areas. The lower limit applies if the driver has held his driving licence for less than two years. Fines are on the spot and if caught speeding at 25kmh (15mph) above the speed limit you may also have your driving licence confiscated immediately.

Driving is on the right-hand side in France. While driving, take particular care at junctions. The rule of giving right of way to traffic coming from the right can still apply (*Priorité à Droite*). A yellow diamond sign indicates you have priority. On a roundabout you generally give priority to traffic coming from the left. One word of warning, if a driver flashes his headlights in France it generally indicates that he has priority and that you should give way. This is contrary to the standard practice (but not the law) in the UK.

Further up-to-date advice on travelling abroad can be obtained from the Foreign and Commonwealth Office (www.fco.gov.uk).

Some of the tours in this book do use some narrow roads, so take care when driving, parking and walking. When travelling please be courteous to the local people and show respect when looking about near their property or land. Please do not trespass.

Another cost-effective way of travelling to, or around, Normandy is to use one of the many battlefield tour coach travel companies. With experienced guides to enhance your tour of the area these can provide an invaluable insight into Normandy landings. Leger Holidays, offer many tours, some conducted by authors who write for the *Battleground Europe* Series. A brochure can be obtained by calling 0845 408 07 69 or by visiting their website (www.leger.co.uk).

For more personal tours, in smaller groups, these can be arranged on a daily basis. These tours can also include visits to areas not open to the general public. Contact Stuart Robertson via his website at **www.normandybattletours.com**.

There are plenty of hotels to choose from in this area of Normandy, though remember that these are always busy around each anniversary. I have often used the Hôtel Restaurant Kyriad Caen-sud (www.kyriad.com), 698, route de Falaise, 14123 IFS Caen. Tel: 0033 (0)2.31.78.38.38. This hotel is situated on junction (*sortie*) No. 13 of the Caen southern ring road (*péripherique Sud*), from where you can join the A13 (*Autoroute de Normandie*) which leads to the D515 and D514 to Bénouville.

Alternatively other accommodation can be found online on the official website of the French Tourist Office (www.francetourism.com) and French Government Tourist Office (wwww.franceguide.com). Local tourist information can also be found at the following regional and county tourist boards and tourist offices (*Office de Tourisme* or *Syndicat d'Initiative*): Normandy Tourist Board (www.normandie-tourisme.fr), Calvados Tourist Board (www.calvados-tourisme.com), Cabourg Tourist Office (www.cabourg.net), and Caen Tourist Office (www.tourisme.caen.fr).

To make the best use of this guide it would be of benefit to read it before you travel. This will help you become familiar with the operation and objectives given to the 6th Airborne Division as well as highlighting the significance of the local features and the area in general. While on your tour this guide will provide a ready reference and direction to the villages, memorials and cemeteries as well as a detailed description of the battles.

Since much of the story is told in the words of the veterans themselves it will also vividly recreate the emotional turmoil of excitement, uncertainty, comradeship and horrors that face men in times of war. Above all, it is my intention that this guide will allow you to better understand the reason why the sacrifices made by these young men so many years ago should never be forgotten; along with the hope that, while that memory remains fresh, another generation of mothers, fathers, daughters and sons need never again experience the indiscriminate killing, and waste, of total war.

Hitler on a tour of his Atlantic Wall.

GLOSSARY

The following abbreviations cover not only abbreviations that may be found in this publication, but also abbreviations that are used on the many memorials, plaques, headstones and museum information boards in this area of Normandy. Some of these abbreviations are non-standard; others have been compiled with the use of the following documents and publications: 6th Airborne Division War Diaries. The War Office, FSPB, Pam No. 2 (1940). The War Office, TM 30-410 Handbook on the British Army (1943). The War Office, Vocabulary of German Military Terms and Abbreviations (1943). Lee, Defence Terminology, Brassey's UK (1991) and The Oxford Dictionary of Abbreviations (1992).

A

AA	Anti-Aircraft
AAC	Army Air Corps
AA & QMG	Assistant Adjutant and Quartermaster General
AARR	Armoured Airborne Reconnaissance Regiment
Ab or A/b	Airborne
ack-ack	Anti-Aircraft fire
ADC	Aide de Camp
Adj	Adjutant
Adm	Administration
ADMS	Assistant Director of Medical Services
ADS	Advance Dressing Station
Adv	Advance
AFC	Air Force Cross
Airldg	Airlanding
Airfd	Airfield
AKC	Associate of King's College, London
Amb	Ambulance
Amn	Ammunition
Armd	Armoured
Artillerie	German for Artillery
Arty	Artillery
ASN	Airborne Support Net
Att	Attached
A Tk	Anti-tank

B

Bangalore Torpedo	Piping filled with explosive, used to blow gaps in barbed wire
Bataillon	German for Battalion
Bde	Brigade
Bdr	Bombardier, Royal Artillery's equivalent of corporal
BM	Brigade Major
BFMC	*Battalion de Fusiliers Marins Commando* (French Commandos)
Bn	Battalion
BOWO	Brigade Ordnance Warrant Officer
BRASCO	Brigade Royal Army Service Corps Officer
Br	Bridge
Bren	.303in British Light Machine-Gun capable of firing 500 rounds per minute
Brig	Brigadier

BST	..	..	..	British Summer Time
Bty	..	..	..	Battery

C

Capt	..	..	..	Captain
Cas	..	..	..	Casualty
CB (Award)	..	..	..	Companion of the (Order of the) Bath
CB (War Diary)	..	..	Counter Battery
CCS	..	..	..	Casualty Clearing Station
Cdn	..	..	..	Canadian
Cdo	..	..	..	Commando
CF	..	..	..	Chaplain of the Forces
C in C	..	..	..	Commander-in-Chief
cm	..	..	..	Centimetre (Metric measurement of length = 10mm or 0.3973in)
CO	..	..	..	Commanding Officer
Col	..	..	..	Colonel
Comd	..	..	..	Commander
Comn	..	..	..	Communication
Comp	..	..	..	Composite
coup de main	..	..	..	A sudden blow or attack
Coy	..	..	..	Company
Cpl	..	..	..	Corporal
CRA	..	..	..	Commander Royal Artillery
CRASC	..	..	..	Commander Royal Army Service Corps
CRE	..	..	..	Commander Royal Engineers
CREME	..	..	..	Commander Royal Electrical Mechanical Engineers
CSM	..	..	..	Company Sergeant Major
CSMI	..	..	..	Company Sergeant Major Instructor
CSMPTI	..	..	..	Company Sergeant Major Physical Training Instructor
CWGC	..	..	..	Commonwealth War Graves Commission
cwt	..	..	..	hundredweight (Imperial measurement of weight = 112lbs or 50.8023kg)

D

DAA & QMG	..	..	..	Deputy Assistant Adjutant and Quartermaster General
DCM	..	..	..	Distinguished Conduct Medal
Def	..	..	..	Defence
Det	..	..	..	Detachment
Devons	..	..	..	The Devonshire Regiment
Div	..	..	..	Division
DSO	..	..	..	Distinguished Service Order
DZ	..	..	..	Drop Zone

E

E	..	..	..	Engineer
ENSA	..	..	..	Entertainment National Service Association
Estd	..	..	..	Established
EUREKA	..	..	..	A radar beacon used by the pathfinders to mark the DZ/LZ

F

Fallschirmjäger	..	..	German for Paratrooper
Fd	..	..	Field
FDL	..	..	Forward Defended Locality
Feldwebel	..	..	German Army rank of Sergeant
Festung Europa	..	..	Fortress Europe, aka Atlantic Wall
Flak	..	..	German for Anti-Aircraft fire
Fm	..	..	Farm
FO or F/O	..	..	Flying Officer
FOB	..	..	Forward Observer Bombardment
FOO	..	..	Forward Observation Officer
FOS	..	..	Forward Observation Section
FS or F/S	..	..	Flight Sergeant
ft	..	..	Foot (feet) (Imperial measurement of length = 12ins or 0.3048m)
FUP	..	..	Forming Up Point
Fwd	..	..	Forward

G

Generalfeldmarschall	..	..	German Army rank of Field Marshal
Generalleutnant	..	..	German Army rank of Lieutenant General
Generalmajor	..	..	German Army rank of Major General
Generaloberst	..	..	German Army rank of General
Gammon Grenade	..	..	No 82 Grenade, consisted of a bag and igniter, into which a variable amount of plastic explosives could be packed. An ideal weapon for mouse holing or disabling tracks of armoured vehicles.
Gnr	..	..	Gunner, Royal Artillery's equivalent rank of Private
GOC	..	..	General Officer Commanding
GOLD	..	..	Codename for one of the five designated landing beaches in Normandy
Gefreiter	..	..	German Army rank of Lance Corporal
GSO	..	..	General Staff Officer (graded 1-3)

H

Hauptfeldwebel	..	..	German Army rank of Company Sergeant Major
Hauptmann	..	..	German Army rank of Captain
HE	..	..	High Explosives
Hitlerjugend	..	..	Hitler Youth – name for *12 SS Panzer Division*
HQ	..	..	Headquarters
Hvy	..	..	Heavy

I

I (also Int)	..	..	Intelligence
IA	..	..	Inter-Allied
In(s)	..	..	Inch(es) (Imperial measurement of length = 25.4mm)
Ind	..	..	Independent
Infanterie	..	..	German for Infantry
Int (also I)	..	..	Intelligence
IO	..	..	Intelligence Officer

J

Junc	..	..	..	Junction
JUNO	..	..	..	Codename for one of the five designated landing beaches in Normandy

K

KA	..	..	..	Killed Arnhem (Operation MARKET)
kg	..	..	..	kilogram(s) (Metric measurement of weight = 2.2046lbs)
KIA	..	..	..	Killed in Action
KN	..	..	..	Killed Normandy
km	..	..	..	kilometre(s) (Metric measurement of length = 1000m or 0.6214miles)
kmh	..	..	..	Kilometre per hour (Metric measurement of speed = 0.6214mph)
KOSB	..	..	..	The King's Own Scottish Borderers
KR	..	..	..	Killed Rhine (Operation VARSITY)
KStJ	..	..	..	Knight of St John
KwK	..	..	..	*Kampfwagenkanone*, German tank gun, sometimes used as a static anti-tank gun on the Atlantic Wall

L

LAD	..	..	..	Light Aid Detachment
lb(s)				pound(s) (Imperial measurement of weight = 0.4536kg)
L Bdr	..	..	..	Lance Bombardier
L Cpl or L/Cpl	..	..	..	Lance Corporal
L Sgt	..	..	..	Lance Sergeant
Leutnant	..	..	..	German Army rank of 2nd Lieutenant
Lieut	..	..	..	Lieutenant
LMG	..	..	..	Light Machine-Gun
Lt	..	..	..	Light or Lieutenant
Lt Col	..	..	..	Lieutenant Colonel
Lt Kol Arty	..	..	..	*Luitenant Kolonel Artillerie* (Dutch rank of Lt Col)
Lt Gen	..	..	..	Lieutenant General
LZ	..	..	..	Landing Zone

M

m	..	..	..	metre(s) (Metric measurement of length = 100cm or 3.2808ft)
Major	..	..	..	German Army rank of Major
Maj Gen	..	..	..	Major General
MALLARD	..	..	..	Codename for glider landings at LZ N & W at 2100hrs on the evening of 6 June 1944
Mauser	..	..	..	German 7.92mm Rifle
MC	..	..	..	Military Cross
M/C	..	..	..	Motorcycle
MDS	..	..	..	Main Dressing Station
ME	..	..	..	Messerschmitt, German aircraft manufacturer
Med	..	..	..	Medium
MG	..	..	..	Machine-Gun
MID	..	..	..	Mentioned in Despatches
MIKE	..	..	..	Codename for one of four sections of JUNO Beach

miles	..	..	..	mile(s) (Imperial measurement of length = 1760yds or 1.6093km)
Mk	..	..	..	Mark
mm	..	..	..	millimetre (Metric measurement of length = 0.0394in)
MM	..	..	..	Military Medal
MMG	..	..	..	Medium Machine-Gun
Mn	..	..	..	minutes
MO	..	..	..	Medical Officer
mouse holing	..	..	..	Term used for making an internal passage between two buildings.
mph	..	..	..	Miles per hour (Imperial measurement of speed = 1.6093kmh)

N

NAAFI	..	..	..	Navy, Army and Airforce Institutes
NAN	..	..	..	Codename for one of the four sections of JUNO Beach
NCO	..	..	..	Non-Commissioned Officer
NEPTUNE	..	..	..	Codename for assault phase of OVERLORD

O

OB	..	..	..	*Oberbefehlshaber* (Commander-in-Chief)
OBOE	..	..	..	RAF radar precision bombing system
Oberleutnant	..	..	..	German Army rank of Lieutenant
Obergefreiter	..	..	..	German Army Rank of Senior Lance Corporal
Obershütze	..	..	..	German Army rank of Private (also *Schütze*)
Oberstleutnant	..	..	..	German Army Rank of Lieutenant Colonel
OC	..	..	..	Officer Commanding
Offr	..	..	..	Officer
O Group	..	..	..	Orders Group
Op	..	..	..	Operation
OP	..	..	..	Observation Post
Ops	..	..	..	Operations (Staff Branch)
OR (also Ors)	..	..	..	Other Ranks
Ord Fd Park	..	..	..	Ordnance Field Park
OT	..	..	..	*Organisation Todt*, German construction organisation
OVERLORD	..	..	..	Codename for the invasion of Normandy
Oxf Bucks	..	..	..	The Oxfordshire and Buckinghamshire (52nd Foot) Light Infantry

P

PaK	..	..	..	*Panzerabwehrkanone*, German mobile or static anti-tank gun
Panzer	..	..	..	German for Armour
Panzerfaust	..	..	..	German hand-held anti-tank weapon
Para	..	..	..	Parachute Battalion (ie 7 Para, 9 Para etc)
Para Bde	..	..	..	Parachute Brigade
pdr	..	..	..	Pounder, as in the British 25pdr field gun
Ph	..	..	..	Phase
PIAT	..	..	..	Projector Infantry Anti-Tank (British hand-held anti-tank weapon)
Pl	..	..	..	Platoon

P/O	..	..	..	Pilot Officer
Posn	..	..	..	Position
POW (also PW)	..	..	..	Prisoner of War
Pk	..	..	..	Park
PRA	..	..	..	Parachute Regimental Association
Pro Coy	..	..	..	Provost Company
Pt	..	..	..	Point
Pte	..	..	..	Private, the lowest rank in the British Army
PW (or POW)	..	..	..	Prisoner of War
Pz	..	..	..	Panzer
Pz Gren	..	..	..	*Panzergrenadier*, infantry of a *Panzer Division*

Q

QLB	..	..	..	Quad Long Bofors
QM	..	..	..	Quartermaster
QUEEN	..	..	..	Codename for one of the four sections of SWORD Beach

R

RA	..	..	..	Royal Artillery
RAC	..	..	..	Royal Armoured Corps
RAMC	..	..	..	Royal Army Medical Corps
RAP	..	..	..	Regimental Aid Post
RASC	..	..	..	Royal Army Service Corps
Rd	..	..	..	Road
RE	..	..	..	Royal Engineers
Recce	..	..	..	Reconnaissance or Reconnoitre
Ref	..	..	..	Reference
Regt	..	..	..	Regiment
REME	..	..	..	Royal Electrical Mechanical Engineers
Rep	..	..	..	Representative
Rfts	..	..	..	Reinforcements
RHQ	..	..	..	Regimental Headquarters
Rly	..	..	..	Railway
RM	..	..	..	Royal Marine
RMO	..	..	..	Regimental Medical Officer
ROGER	..	..	..	Codename for one of the four sections of SWORD Beach
Rommel's Asparagus		..		Name given to the anti-airborne defence poles set up in open fields
RSM	..	..	..	Regimental Sergeant Major
RUR	..	..	..	The Royal Ulster Rifles
RV	..	..	..	Rendezvous, the point at which troops would gather before moving to their Objective

S

SAS	..	..	..	Special Air Service
Schmeisser	..	..	..	German 9mm sub-machine gun
Schütze	..	..	..	German Army rank of Private (also *Obershütze*)
Sec	..	..	..	Section
Sgt	..	..	..	Sergeant
Sigmn	..	..	..	Signalman
Sigs	..	..	..	Signals
SL	..	..	..	Start Line
SNAFU	..	..	..	Acronym for Situation Normal All F****d Up

SOE	..	..	..	Special Operations Executive
Spandau	..	..	..	German 7.92mm MG34 or MG42 machine-gun
SP	..	..	..	Self-Propelled (gun)
Spr	..	..	..	Sapper, RE equivalent rank of Private
Sq	..	..	..	Square
Sqn	..	..	..	Squadron
SS	..	..	..	Special Service
SS	..	..	..	Steam Ship
SS (German)	..	..	..	*Schutzstaffel* (*Waffen-SS*) armed defence echelon,
SSM	..	..	..	Staff Sergeant Major
S Sgt or S/Sgt	..	..	..	Staff Sergeant
Stabsfeldwebel	..	..	..	German Army rank of Staff Sergeant
Sta	..	..	..	Station
Sten	..	..	..	British 9mm sub-machine gun
Stick	..	..	..	One aircraft load of parachute troops, to be dropped in one run over one dropzone
Str	..	..	..	Strength
SWORD	..	..	..	Codename for one of the five designated landing beaches in Normandy

T

TAF	..	..	..	Tactical Air Force
TD	..	..	..	Territorial (Army Efficiency) Decoration
Tks	..	..	..	Tanks
THOMAS	..	..	..	Codename for the green light location devices fitted to parachute containers
ton(s)	..	..	..	Ton(s) (Imperial measurement of weight = 20cwt or 1.0160 tonnes)
tonnes	..	..	..	Tonne(s) (Metric measurement of weight = 1000kg or 0.9842 UK tons)
TONGA	..	..	..	Codename for the first three waves of glider landings at LZ X, Y, K, V & N prior to seaborne landings
Tp	..	..	..	Troop

U

unkn	..	..	..	unknown
Unterfeldwebel	..	..	..	German Army rank of Corporal
Unteroffizier	..	..	..	German Army NCO rank

W

Warwicks	..	..	..	The Royal Warwickshire Regiment
WC or W/C	..	..	..	Wing Commander
Wehrmacht	..	..	..	German Armed Forces
Wkshop	..	..	..	Workshop
WO or W/O	..	..	..	Warrant Officer
WO	..	..	..	War Office
W Y	..	..	..	Worcestershire Yeomanry

Y

yds	..	..	..	yards (Imperial measurement of length = 3ft or 0.9144m)
Yeo	..	..	..	Yeomanry

Misc

2ic (or 2i/c)	..	..	..	Second in Command

25

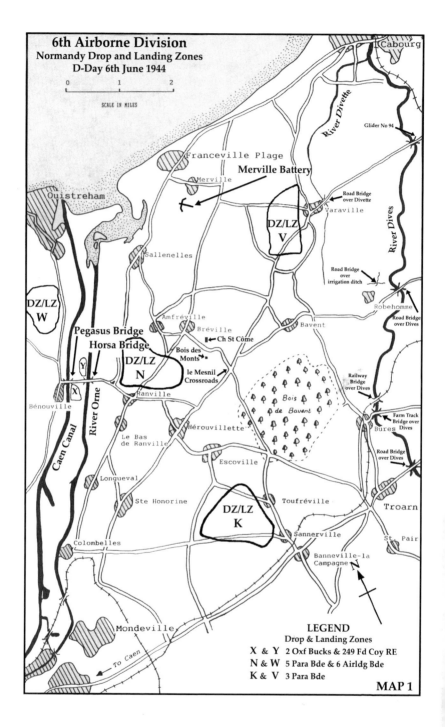

6th Airborne Division
Normandy Drop and Landing Zones
D-Day 6th June 1944

0   1   2

SCALE IN MILES

Cabourg

River Divette

Glider No 94

Franceville Plage

Merville

Merville Battery

Road Bridge over Divette

Varaville

DZ/LZ V

Ouistreham

Sallenelles

Road Bridge over irrigation ditch

Robehomme

Road Bridge over Dives

River Dives

DZ/LZ W

Amfréville

Bréville

Bavent

Pegasus Bridge
Horsa Bridge

Ch St Côme

Bois des Monts

DZ/LZ N

le Mesnil Crossroads

Bois de Bavent

Railway Bridge over Dives

Y

X

Ranville

Farm Track Bridge over Dives

Bures

Bénouville

Hérouvillette

Caen Canal

River Orne

Le Bas de Ranville

Road Bridge over Dives

Longueval

Escoville

Ste Honorine

DZ/LZ K

Toufréville

Troarn

Sannerville

St. Pair

Colombelles

Banneville-la Campagne

N

Mondeville

To Caen

LEGEND
Drop & Landing Zones

X & Y   2 Oxf Bucks & 249 Fd Coy RE
N & W   5 Para Bde & 6 Airldg Bde
K & V   3 Para Bde

MAP 1

CHAPTER ONE

PLANNING THE INVASION

THE ALLIED PLAN

Operation OVERLORD involved the initial landing of six divisions – three American, two British and one Canadian – on five beaches over a 50-mile (80.46km) stretch of Normandy coastline between Quinéville on the east coast of the Côtentin Peninsular and Ouistreham at the mouth of the River Orne. It had been decided that the best time to land on the beaches was just after first light in the morning, just below mid tide, and on a flooding tide, as this gave the advantage that most of the beach defences would be seen and could therefore be destroyed or avoided. Low tide would have created too large an area of open ground for the troops to cross, up to 600 yards (549m) in places, making the beaches a killing field. High tide would leave the beach defences of mines and obstacles undetectable and also leave too small an area for the troops to disembark and organise themselves.

Due to the distance involved, and the run of the tide, the First (US) Army were due to land first on UTAH and OMAHA Beaches at 0630hrs. These would be followed by the Second (British) Army at GOLD and SWORD Beaches at 0725hrs, and

Pre-invasion exercises at a Training Centre of Combined Operation Command. RAF Mustangs come in low over landing craft in a simulated attack.

JUNO Beach at 0750hrs.

In order to protect the outer flanks of the seaborne invasion and help disable the German Atlantic Wall from the rear, an additional assault of three airborne divisions, two American and one British, would precede the beach assault at just after midnight on the night of the 5/6 June, 1944. On the right flank

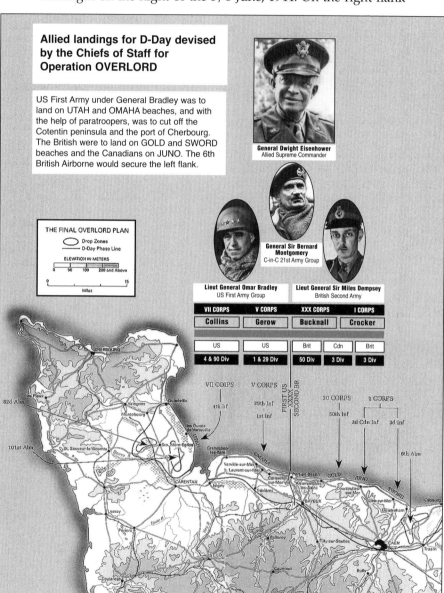

Allied landings for D-Day devised by the Chiefs of Staff for Operation OVERLORD

US First Army under General Bradley was to land on UTAH and OMAHA beaches, and with the help of paratroopers, was to cut off the Cotentin peninsula and the port of Cherbourg. The British were to land on GOLD and SWORD beaches and the Canadians on JUNO. The 6th British Airborne would secure the left flank.

General Dwight Eisenhower
Allied Supreme Commander

General Sir Bernard Montgomery
C-in-C 21st Army Group

Lieut General Omar Bradley
US First Army Group

Lieut General Sir Miles Dempsey
British Second Army

VII CORPS	V CORPS	XXX CORPS	I CORPS
Collins	Gerow	Bucknall	Crocker
US	US	Brit	Cdn	Brit
4 & 90 Div	1 & 29 Div	50 Div	3 Div	3 Div

THE FINAL OVERLORD PLAN
Drop Zones
D-Day Phase Line
ELEVATION IN METERS
0   50   100   200 and Above

15,000 troops of the 82nd (All American) and 101st (Screaming Eagles) US Airborne Divisions would land on the Côtentin Peninsula and, on the left flank, approximately 12,000 troops of the British 6th Airborne Division would come to ground and secure an area around and between the Caen Canal and River Dives (see Map 1).

After the firm establishment of a bridgehead on the beaches and a link-up of the British and Canadian armies with the 6th Airborne Division, General Montgomery planned to use the threat of a breakout in the 6th Airborne Division sector to draw and contain enemy reserves on the eastern flank.

> *My plan was to make the breakout on the western flank, using for this task the American armies under General Bradley, and to pivot the whole front on Caen. The American breakout thrust was to be delivered southwards down to the Loire and then to be developed eastwards in a wide sweep up to the Seine about Paris. This movement was designed to cut off all the enemy forces south of the Seine, over which river the bridges were to be destroyed by air action.*[1]
>
> GENERAL MONTGOMERY, COMMANDER, 21ST ARMY GROUP

Within the first forty-eight hours of the invasion General Eisenhower, the Supreme Commander of the Allied Expeditionary Force, planned to land, by sea, 176,475 men along with 20,111 vehicles (these included 1,500 tanks, 5,000 tracked vehicles, 3,000 guns and 10,611 assorted vehicles from jeeps to bulldozers). In total, by D-Day,* thirty-seven divisions (twenty-three infantry, ten armoured and four airborne) were to be available in Britain to carry out the mission of invading north-west Europe. The use of 5,000 ships and 4,000 additional landing craft and air cover supplied by 171 fighter squadrons[2] ensured that D-Day was set to be the greatest combined operation ever attempted.

Subsequent books in this *Battleground Europe* series cover, in detail, the beach and American airborne landings in Normandy.

---

* The term D-Day is actually standard army nomenclature to signify the day a military operation begins. The letter D does not represent anything other than to emphasise the word Day. The first recorded use was in 1918 in Field Order No. 8, First Army, Allied Expeditionary Force. Such an expression allows the build-up and operation phases to be measured in days (i.e. D-1, D+1, etc.). Similarly, H-Hour is used to represent the actual time on D-Day that an operation begins. However, because of the scale of the Normandy landings the term D-Day has now passed into common usage to represent the events of 6 June 1944 and Operation OVERLORD (see The Oxford English Dictionary).

This book *Pegasus Bridge & Horsa Bridge* and the accompanying book in this series, *Merville Battery & The Dives Bridges*, will concentrate on the objectives and operations of the British 6th Airborne Division; looking in detail at the events that surrounded their landings on the left flank of the invasion force on 6 June 1944.

FORMATION OF THE 6th AIRBORNE DIVISION

Orders were issued by the War Office on 23 April 1943 for the formation of the 6th Airborne Division.[3] On 7 May 1943, Major General Richard Gale, the appointed commander, arrived at Syrencot House near Durrington, on Salisbury Plain in Wiltshire and formed the divisional headquarters (HQ). Meanwhile 6 Airlanding Brigade (6 Airldg Bde) HQ was formed at Amesbury. It was around this time that the decision was made that the 1st Airborne Division sign – Bellerophon mounted astride the winged horse Pegasus, the first recorded airborne warrior – should be adopted as the airborne forces sign. This now famous emblem was also supported by a divisional motto that Major General Richard Gale placed in one of the first copies of Divisional Routine Orders – GO TO IT.

This motto will be adopted by the 6th Airborne Division and as such should be remembered by all ranks in action against the enemy, in training, and during the day to day routine duties.

In this wise and from these beginnings was the 6th Airborne Division born.[4]

MAJOR GENERAL RICHARD GALE, GOC 6TH AIRBORNE DIVISION

Major General Richard Gale.

Although 6th Airborne Division was in fact Britain's second airborne division, the number six was chosen in order to mislead enemy intelligence. From May to 22 September the division grew in size to its full strength; then on 23 December 1943, the division was ordered to complete its training and mobilize in preparation for operational duty by 1 February, 1944. In less than nine months after its initial formation the 6th Airborne Division was assembled and ready for active service. Considering that

Right : **British paratroopers check their equipment before making a practise jump.**

Lieutenant General F. 'Boy' Browning.

some 12,000 men were involved, it was a remarkable achievement. Sixteen days later Lieutenant General Frederick 'Boy' Browning, commander of I Airborne Corps, briefed Major General Gale on the role his division would play in the Normandy invasion.

So it came about that on the 24th February, the 6th Airborne Division was definitely placed under command of the I British Corps for Operation OVERLORD. For planning, a small party consisting of myself,

Bobby Bray, my GSO 1, Lacoste, my GSO 2, Intelligence, one GSO 3, Shamus Hickie... my CRA and Frank Lowman my CRE with the chief clerk went up to I Corps Headquarters in Ashley Gardens, London.

It was here that I received my orders and here that we worked out our outline plan. A plan which, save for very minor modifications, we never altered.[5]

MAJOR GENERAL RICHARD GALE, GOC 6TH AIRBORNE DIVISION

OBJECTIVES OF THE 6th AIRBORNE DIVISION

The 6th Airborne Division had three primary tasks[6] as part of their role in covering the eastern flank of the invasion:

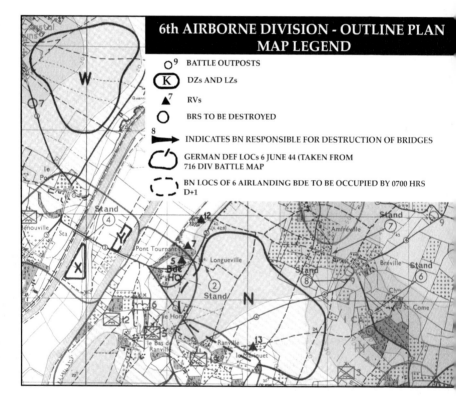

6th AIRBORNE DIVISION - OUTLINE PLAN MAP LEGEND

- O^9 BATTLE OUTPOSTS
- (K)   DZs AND LZs
- ▲[7]   RVs
- O   BRS TO BE DESTROYED
- [8] ►   INDICATES BN RESPONSIBLE FOR DESTRUCTION OF BRIDGES
- GERMAN DEF LOCs 6 JUNE 44 (TAKEN FROM 716 DIV BATTLE MAP
- BN LOCS OF 6 AIRLANDING BDE TO BE OCCUPIED BY 0700 HRS D+1

TASK ONE (see Map 2, page 60)

The bridges over the Caen Canal (Bénouville Bridge) and the River Orne (Ranville Bridge) were to be captured intact in order to allow the rapid deployment of reinforcements from SWORD Beach. This would then greatly help the defence of the bridgehead, which by then would have already been established by the rest of the 6th Airborne Division, so that it could be maintained and exploited. This operation was to be carried out in a *coup de main* glider operation by one reinforced company (six platoons) from B and D Company (Coy) of 2nd Battalion Oxfordshire and Buckinghamshire Light Infantry (2 Oxf Bucks) of 5 Parachute Brigade (5 Para Bde).

Under the command of Major John Howard the infantry were accompanied by thirty engineers from No. 2 Platoon of 249 Field Company Royal Engineers (Fd Coy RE). All were due to land at Landing Zone (LZ) X & Y at approximately 0020hrs in six gliders.

Simultaneously, three advance parties of pathfinders from the 22nd (Independent) Parachute Company [22 (Ind) Para Coy] would drop at Landing Zone/Drop Zone (LZ/DZ) N, V & K and mark the LZ/DZs for the main body of 3 Parachute Brigade (3 Para Bde) at DZs V & K and 5 Para Bde at DZ N at 0050hrs.

5 Para Bde, commanded by Brigadier Nigel Poett, would then reinforce the *coup de main* party and secure and hold the area around the bridge at Bénouville (today known as Pegasus Bridge) and at Ranville (today known as Horsa Bridge) until relieved by a battalion

Brigadier J.H.N. Poett.

from 8 Infantry Brigade (8 Inf Bde) of the British 3rd Infantry Division who would be landing on SWORD Beach at 0730hrs.

TASK TWO (see Map 1, page 26)
The destruction of the coastal gun emplacement known as the Merville Battery had to be achieved, as it was believed that each of the four casemates would contain 150mm (5.91in) calibre howitzers. Such weapons potentially had a range of over 20,000 yards (18,288m), some 11.36 miles (18.29km) and would wreak havoc among the assault craft as they approached the landing beaches. As heavy bombing could not guarantee the destruction of the battery guns, it was ultimately decided that the only way of neutralizing this position was by the use of another *coup de main* operation by the airborne forces.

This operation would involve the landing of three gliders within the German battery perimeter and between the casemates, while the main assault force launched its attack through the perimeter mined and barbed wire defences. This assault was assigned to the 9th Parachute Battalion (9 Para), under the command of Lieutenant Colonel Terence Otway. With 9 Para were a troop of engineers from 591 Parachute Squadron Royal Engineers (591 Para Sqn RE), to help clear the minefields around the battery and destroy the guns in the casemates.

The main assault force of 9 Para were to drop with the rest of 3 Para Bde, less HQ and the 8th Parachute Battalion (8 Para), at DZ/LZ V.

TASK THREE (see Map 1, page 26)
The destruction of four bridges over the River Dives (one near Robehomme, two in Bures-sur-Dives and one near Troarn); one bridge over the River Divette at Varaville and a culvert (small bridge) across an irrigation ditch near Robehomme. This was necessary to delay the advance of enemy reinforcements from the east into the area of operations for 6th Airborne Division.

These tasks would be carried out by the 3rd Parachute Squadron, Royal Engineers (3 Para Sqn RE), under the command of Major Adams 'Tim' Roseveare.

The 1st Canadian Parachute Battalion (1 Cdn Para), under the command of Lieutenant Colonel George Bradbrooke, and No. 3 Troop of 3 Para Sqn RE, were to land at DZ/LZ V. One company and a platoon of 1 Cdn Para were assigned the task of protecting No. 3 Troop 3 Para Sqn RE, while they destroyed the bridge at Varaville and the bridge and culvert near Robehomme.

Meanwhile, Lieutenant Colonel Alastair Pearson's 8 Para were to land some 5 miles (8.05km) south-west at DZ/LZ K. One platoon of paratroopers from 8 Para were then to cover sappers from No. 2 Troop 3 Para Sqn RE, while they destroyed the bridges at Bures-sur-Dives. Meanwhile another platoon from 8 Para were to provide protection for No. 1 Troop 3 Para Sqn RE, as they destroyed the bridge near Troarn.

SECONDARY TASKS
Secondary tasks to be carried out, without prejudice to the three main tasks, were to secure the area between the River Orne and River Dives north of the road (now the D226) that runs, west to east, from Colombelles, through DZ/LZ K, into Sannerville and then on to Troarn (now N175), and to delay any enemy reserves from moving into this area.[7]

REINFORCEMENTS

The first reinforcements would arrive at LZ N at 0320hrs, followed, in the second *coup de main* operation of the night, by a detachment from 9th Parachute Battalion (9 Para) at 0430hrs, who were due to land in three Horsa gliders, inside the 400 square yard (366sq m) area of the Merville Battery. This operation was timed to coincide with the main assault on the position by the rest of 9 Para. It was then planned that No. 4 Commando (4 Cdo), of Lord Lovat's No. 1 Special Service Brigade (1 SS Bde), would land on SWORD Beach at la Bréche at 0820hrs. Also attached to 4 Cdo were No. 1 and No. 8 French Troop of *1er Bataillon de Fusiliers Marins Commando* (1 BFMC). This unit having recently been transferred, on 1 May 1944, from No. 10 (Inter Allied) Commando [10 (IA) Cdo].

RAF reconnaissance photograph taken in March, 1944. Bénouville (Pegasus) Bridge, over the Caen Canal, is in the foreground to the left. Ranville (Horsa) Bridge over the River Orne in the lower right. In the distance at the top is Ouistreham and part of SWORD Beach.

The objective for 4 Cdo was to destroy the coastal defence battery, on the site of the former casino at Riva-Bella in Ouistreham, thereby aiding the landing at 0840hrs of the remaining units of 1 SS Bde and 3rd Infantry Division. Lord Lovat would then lead his men over the 6.5 miles (10.46km) of enemy held territory and form the link-up between the airborne and seaborne troops[8] at approximately H+4 hrs at the captured bridges. They would then move on and patrol an area between Amfréville, the *Château St Côme* and Bavent. The leading elements of 3rd Infantry Division were expected to reach Bénouville by H+5 hours.[9]

At 2100 hrs, on the evening of D-Day, 6 Airldg Bde would make up the final and largest reinforcement by air at LZ/DZ N & W.

The remaining units of the 6th Airborne Division, due to a shortage of suitable planes, gliders and pilots were to arrive by sea between D-Day+1 and D-Day+7. These would include elements of: 2nd Airlanding Light Anti-Aircraft Battery, Royal Artillery (2 Airldg Lt AA Bty RA); 3rd Airlanding Anti-Tank Battery Royal Artillery (3 Airldg A Tk Bty RA), less one troop; 12th Battalion the Devonshire Regiment (12 Devons) less one company; 53rd (Worcestershire Yeomanry) Airlanding Light Regiment [53 (WY) Airldg Lt Regt RA], less the 211th battery; 195th Airlanding Field Ambulance (195 Airldg Fd Amb), less two sections; and other divisional troops.[10] In total some 3,253 troops and 530 vehicles would be landed on QUEEN and ROGER sectors of SWORD Beach, west of Ouistreham and NAN and MIKE sectors of JUNO Beach at Courseulles-sur-Mer.[11]

The task of delivering all the airborne troops to their designated DZs and LZs was given to the squadrons of No. 38 and No. 46 Group, Royal Air Force (RAF).

No. 38 Group RAF had fleets of: Halifaxes of No. 298 & No. 644 Squadrons (Sqns) flying out of Tarrant Rushton; Albemarles of No. 296 & No. 297 Sqns from Brize Norton and No. 295 and No. 570 Sqns from Harwell; Stirlings of No. 196 and No. 299 Sqns from Keevil and No. 190 and No. 620 Sqns from Fairford.

No. 46 Group RAF had fleets of: Dakotas of No. 512 and No. 575 from Broadwell, No. 48 and No. 271 Sqns from Down Ampney and No. 233 Sqn from Blakehill Farm.[12]

The RAF would also tow the Horsa and Hamilcar gliders of No. 1 and No. 2 Wing of the Glider Pilot Regiment. Operation TONGA would be the codename for the night operations on the

5/6 June and Operation MALLARD would be the codename for the resupply mission on the evening of 6 June.

GROUPING

Each parachute brigade had under its command the following units:

3 Para Brigade (DZ/LZ V & K)	**5 Para Brigade** (DZ/LZ N)
Det 22 (Ind) Para Coy	Det 22 (Ind) Para Coy
1 Cdn Para	7 Para
8 Para	12 Para
9 Para	13 Para
4 Airldg A Tk Bty RA (one sec)	3 Airldg A Tk Bty RA (one tp)
3 Para Sqn RE	4 Airldg A Tk Bty RA (less one sec)
591 Para Sqn RE (one tp)	D Coy 2 Oxf Bucks
FOO, 53 (WY) Airldg Lt Regt RA	591 Para Sqn RE (less one tp)
FOB attd 3 Para Bde	FOO 53 (WY) Airldg L Regt RA
224 Para Fd Amb	FOB attd 5 Para Bde
	225 Para Fd Amb
	286 Fd Pk Coy RE (one sec)
	RASC (elements)
	FOB 3 Inf Div

(for complete Order of Battle see Appendix C)

The two parachute brigades also had the use of two cruisers and two destroyers off the coast of Normandy: HMS *Arethusa*, equipped with 6in (152.4mm) guns, and a destroyer for 3 Para Bde; HMS *Mauritius*, equipped with 4.7in (119.38mm) guns, and a destroyer for 5 Para Bde. Four further destroyers were also available for 1 SS Bde. These naval guns could be called upon for artillery support.

The cruiser, HMS *Arethusa*, one of the warships assigned to provide covering fire for the parachute brigades.

A mixed team would make up artillery support for each of the brigades. Army Forward Observer Officers (FOOs) would direct ground artillery fire and army officers trained in naval gunnery procedures, aided by Royal Navy wireless operators, would form Forward Observers Bombardment (FOBs). These teams, dropped with the paratroopers, would use radio contact to control the ships' fire[13] and other ground artillery support. Four FOOs and three FOBs were allotted to both 3 Para Bde and 5 Para Bde. A further eight FOOs were allotted to 6 Airldg Bde.

6th Airlanding Brigade (DZ/LZ N & W)
2 Oxf Bucks (less six pl)
1 RUR
A Coy 12 Devons
6 AARR
211 Airldg Lt Bty RA
249 Fd Coy RE
195 Airldg Fd Amb (two sec)

Landing by sea on D+1
12 Devons (less A Coy)
53 (WY) Airldg Lt Regt RA (less one bty)
3 Airldg A Tk Bty RA (less one tp)
2 Airldg Lt AA Bty RA
195 Airldg Fd Amb (less two sec)
210 Airldg L Bty RA

SUMMARY OF ORDER FOR AIRBORNE LANDINGS
For the two airborne operations, Operation TONGA and Operation MALLARD the parachute drops and glider landings were divided into four waves using 266 paratrooper carrying aircraft and 352 gliders with tugs. Please note: the nominal roll for the Glider Pilot Regiment indicates that there were 352 gliders involved in operations. Records for the 6th Airborne Division account for only 344 gliders. Therefore, eight Horsa gliders, from the total believed to have been involved in the third and fourth wave of operations, are not accounted for in the following summary.

Operation TONGA

First Wave

Time	DZ/LZ	Units	Aircraft
0020hrs	X & Y	D & B Coy 2 Oxf Bucks	6 Horsas + tugs
	N	Pathfinders	2 Albemarles
	N	Adv Party 5 Para Bde HQ	1 Albemarle
	N	Adv Party 7 Para	1 Albemarle
	N	Adv Party 13 Para	3 Albemarles
	V	Pathfinders	2 Albemarles
	V	Adv Party 3 Para Bde	2 Albemarles
	V	C Coy 1 Cdn Para	12 Albemarles
	K	Pathfinders	2 Albemarles
	K	Adv Party 8 Para	2 Albemarles

Second Wave

Time	DZ/LZ	Units	Aircraft
0045hrs	V	HQ 3 Para Bde	2 Horsas +tugs
	V	9 Para	2 Horsas + tugs
	V	591 Para Sqn RE	1 Horsa + tug
	V	1 Cdn Para	1 Horsa + tug
	V	224 Para Fd Amb	3 Horsas + tugs
	V	Det 4 Airldg A Tk Bty RA	2 Horsas + tugs
	K	8 Para, 3 Para Sqn RE, RAMC & RASC	6 Horsas + tugs
0050hrs	N	5 Para Bde	83 Stirlings + 27 Dakotas,19 Albemarles & 2 unkn. para aircraft
0117hrs	N	Adv party HQ 6 Ab Div	2 Stirlings
	V	HQ 3 Para Bde	7 Dakotas
	V	3 Para Bde (less 8 Para)	56 Dakotas
	V	3 Para Sqn RE	3 Dakotas
	V	224 Para Fd Amb	3 Dakotas
	K	8 Para	31 Dakotas
	K	3 Para Sqn RE	6 Dakotas

Albemarle.

Stirling.
Dakota C-47.

Third Wave

The nominal role for the Glider Pilot Regiment lists 216 gliders destined for LZ N and 110 gliders for LZ W. However, 6th Airborne Division records indicate that only 202 gliders were destined for LZ N but that 116 gliders were destined for LZ W. This discrepancy in official records therefore does not allow the actual number of gliders destined for each of these two LZs, in the third and fourth waves, to be accurately determined.

Time	DZ/LZ	Units	Aircraft
0320hrs	N	HQ 6 Ab Div, RE & FOOs	44 Horsas + tugs
	N	4 Airldg A Tk Bty RA	20 Horsas + 4 Hamilcars + tugs
0430hrs	Merville	Det from 9 Para	3 Horsas + Albemarle tugs

Operation MALLARD

Fourth Wave

Time	DZ/LZ	Units	Aircraft
2051hrs	N	HQ 6 Airldg Bde	15 Horsas + tugs
2123hrs	N	1 RUR	70 Horsas + tugs
	N	6 Ab Div Armd Recce Regt	19 Horsas + tugs & 26 Hamilcars + Halifax tugs
	N	3 Airldg Anti-Tank Bty RA	4 Hamilcars + Halifax tugs
	W	2 Oxf Bucks (less D Coy)	65 Horsas + tugs
	W	195 Airldg Fd Amb	6 Horsas + tugs
	W	716 Ab Lt Comp Coy RASC	10 Horsas + tugs
	W	211 Airldg Bty RA	27 Horsas + tugs
	W	A Coy 12 Devons	8 Horsas + tugs

Before we consider the most obvious danger that faced the men of 6th Airborne Division – the strength of the German defences in Normandy – it is important to bear in mind a few of the other hazards that faced the airborne troops as they went into battle. For gliderborne troops this took the form of the aircraft itself.

40

The Horsa Airspeed AS I glider was a plywood and fabric construction which offered very little protection from anti-aircraft or machine-gun fire. The glider was fitted with a removable undercarriage which would sometimes become detached if landing on uneven ground (which was often the case), leaving the glider to land on its central skid.

As the floor of the aircraft could well disintegrate on landing, the passengers, up to thirty fully equipped troops, would wear a lap belt and brace themselves by linking arms or putting their arms around each others' shoulders and then lifting their feet up off the floor in anticipation of the landing. This, at around 90mph (145kmh), proved to be a nerve-wracking experience for all concerned.

The glider pilots themselves were even more exposed and, in the event of hitting any ground obstacles such as 'Rommel's Asparagus', trees, a ditch or indeed another crashed glider, the perspex and wooden nose of the aircraft offered almost no protection on impact.

The Horsa was also used for transporting pieces of equipment such as Jeeps, motorcycles and 6-pounder (2.25in/57mm) anti-

A Tetrarch tank, used by 6 AARR, exiting a Hamilcar glider during a training exercise. Thirty-four Hamilcars were used on D-Day.

Workhorse of the British airborne forces – the Horsa glider.

tank guns; from which there was always a danger of the cargo breaking loose under the impact of a rough landing.

The Hamilcar, could carry a payload up to 17,500lbs (7,938kg), some 7.8 tons (7.9 tonnes), the equivalent of its own weight. It was used to transport larger pieces of artillery and armoured vehicles such as the Tetrarch tank

British glider pilots, once on the ground, fought alongside the airborne infantry. They had the added responsibility of safely delivering their comrades unharmed and their equipment undamaged and ready for action.

Pen & Sword Books

FREEPOST SF5

47 Church Street

BARNSLEY

South Yorkshire

S70 2BR

DISCOVER MORE ABOUT MILITARY HISTORY

Pen & Sword Books have over 1500 titles in print covering all aspects of military history on land, sea and air. If you would like to receive more information and special offers on your preferred interests from time to time along with our standard catalogue, please complete your areas of interest below and return this card (no stamp required in the UK). Alternatively, register online at www.pen-and-sword.co.uk. Thank you.

PLEASE NOTE: We do not sell data information to any third party companies

Mr/Mrs/Ms/Other............. Name...

Address...

.... Postcode..............................

Email address..
if you wish to receive our email newsletter, please tick here ❏

PLEASE SELECT YOUR AREAS OF INTEREST

Ancient History	❏	Medieval History	❏	English Civil War	❏
Napoleonic	❏	Pre World War One	❏	World War One	❏
World War Two	❏	Post World War Two	❏	Falklands	❏
Aviation	❏	Maritime	❏	Battlefield Guides	❏
Regimental History	❏	Military Reference	❏	Military Biography	❏

Website: www.pen-and-sword.co.uk ● Email: enquiries@pen-and-sword.co.uk
Telephone: 01226 734555 ● Fax: 01226 734438

used by 6th Airborne Armoured Reconnaissance Regiment (6 AARR).

The tank crews would stay inside the tank for added safety during the flight, which also enabled them to make a quick exit on landing. This was achieved by starting up the engine while still in flight. On landing, the driver would pull a lanyard to disconnect the lashings that held the tank in place. As he drove forward a trip would automatically release the nose of the glider and allow him to drive straight out and into battle, all within fifteen seconds of landing. Naturally, this complicated procedure held built-in potential danger.

Life for the paratroopers was no less dangerous. Exiting their aircraft at an altitude of between 500ft (152m) and 700ft (213m), laden with in excess of 60lbs (27kg) of equipment, they would be on the ground within 25 seconds. In this time they had to check that their parachutes had opened, go through their anti-collision drill, attempt to get their bearings by locating a landmark and then, in the dark and hoping that they would not become snagged in a tree, building or 'Rommel's Asparagus', make a safe landing!

For those carrying a kitbag or weapon valise there was the added difficulty of releasing this bulky item. The kitbag was designed to carry up to 80lbs (36kg) in weight (although this was often exceeded) and was suspended by a 20ft (6m) rope from the parachute harness. The kitbag was initially attached to the paratrooper's right leg. Upon exiting the aircraft, the paratrooper would have to release the kitbag and steadily lower it to the end of its suspension line. If the kitbag was released too quickly the weight of his equipment would cause the rope line to snap and the kitbag would be lost. If the release pins were not freed correctly it would remain attached to the paratrooper's leg and result, almost certainly, in a broken limb upon landing.[14]

Finally, adding to the potential problems of all the aforementioned, the paratroopers and gliderborne troops would also come under fire from German anti-aircraft guns and machine-guns while they descended.

Manhandling a Jeep aboard via the nose of a Horsa. Approximately 350 Horsa gliders were used by the British 6th Airborne Division on D-Day.

CHAPTER TWO

THE GERMAN DEFENCES IN NORMANDY

THE ATLANTIC WALL

Festung Europa, Hitler's Fortress Europe, more commonly known as the Atlantic Wall, was a system of fortifications under the command of *OB West*, *Generalfeldmarschall* von Rundstedt, which was built by the *Organisation Todt* (*OT*) and stretched some 1,700 miles (2,736km) from the Spanish border to the Netherlands. It proved its worth in the failed raid on Dieppe by the Allies in August of 1942. The Nazi Propaganda Minister, Joseph Goebbels, used the statistics gathered from that bloody fiasco as a warning to the Allies of how impregnable the German fortifications were.

Our Atlantic Wall defences are unbreakable. No one can pass them. If they try, results will be like Dieppe.

Joseph Goebbels

From an assault force of over 6,000 British and Canadian troops, Anglo-Canadian

casualties amounted to 3,613.[1] Records for German casualties, by comparison, show fewer than 600 from all their three services.[2] Nevertheless, until *Generalfeldmarschall* Erwin Rommel, was appointed Inspector General of the Atlantic Wall on 21 November 1943, the coastal defences were, in most places, little more than a propaganda myth.

With manpower constantly being drained to resupply exhausted divisions on the Eastern Front, von Rundstedt believed that the Allies could not be prevented from landing and that they possessed a strategic flexibility that could not be countered by a static defence system. He therefore concentrated most of his defences around the Pas de Calais, Cherbourg, Brest and the mouths of the River Somme and River Seine with the intention of denying the Allies the use of any of the major ports. Without a port it was hoped that the invading army would be denied the opportunity to resupply quickly and it was von Rundstedt's plan then to use his mobile reserves to drive the Allies back into the sea before a sizeable bridgehead could be established.[3]

Just as the defending force has gathered valuable experience from Dieppe, so has the assaulting force. He will not do it like this a second time.
Generalfeldmarschall von Rundstedt

The enemy must be annihilated before he reaches our battlefield. We must stop him in the water, destroying all his equipment while it is still afloat.
Generalfeldmarschall Erwin Rommel.

Rommel, however, disagreed with von Rundstedt and believed that the invasion force must be defeated on the beaches. He appealed to Hitler for command of the Seventh and Fifteenth Armies who defended the coast from north-east France, at the mouth of the River Loire, on to Belgium and through into Holland.[2]

At this stage, in January 1944, much of the coastline of Calvados in Normandy was relatively unfortified.

Although he retained his position as *OB West*, von Rundstedt's command was divided into two army groups with Rommel taking command of Army Group B. Immediately

Rommel began to modify von Rundstedt's plan and Army Group B records show that more than 500,000 foreshore obstacles and 4,000,000 land mines were laid by the end of May 1944. Also, the construction of pillboxes, reinforcement of shelters for anti-tank positions and many other obstacles were in place by June 1944. This would also include (and these would have most effect on the airborne forces) the appearance of anti-glider poles that became known as 'Rommel's Asparagus'. These thick wooden poles, some tipped with explosive shells and trip wires, were placed in many open areas of land within 7 miles (11.27km) of the coastline. At the same time, all low-lying land was flooded and the intermediate areas between were planted with mines.

'Rommel's Asparagus' – anti glider poles.

In June 1944 von Rundstedt had sixty divisions under his command, forty-three of which came under Rommel's Army Group B, with eighteen divisions (fifteen infantry and three armoured) situated between the River Seine and the River Loire. Eisenhower, by comparison, had thirty-seven divisions in Britain, but, due to the logistics involved, all of these could not

Erecting beach obstacles.

Troops put through their paces by NCOs.

A coastal bunker being built.

Rommel visits the building work.

French tank turret becomes a strong point and is then camouflaged with turf.

be brought into action until seven weeks after D-Day.[4]

Three German infantry divisions, *711*, *716* and *352*, and two armoured divisions, *12 SS Panzer* and *21 Panzer*, were all in the vicinity or within reach of the area where the 6th Airborne Division was due to land on the night of the 5/6 June 1944.

711 Infanterie Division was best situated to counter the attack by the 6th Airborne Division. It had an estimated strength of 13,000 troops, twenty anti-tank guns, sixty pieces of field and medium artillery and a French, Renault 35, tank squadron.

716 Infanterie Division was considered a low category division and was situated mainly west of the River Orne with its complement of eight infantry battalions which included two Russian battalions each of a thousand men. It also had artillery support in the form of twenty-four gun-howitzers, twelve medium howitzers and one anti-tank company.

352 Infanterie Division was deployed around Port-en-Bessin and intelligence reports suggested that this was a counter-attack division which, if deployed, could be in the Caen area within eight hours.

SS-*Standartenführer* **Kurt Meyer. 12 SS Panzer Division Hitlerjugend** .

12 SS Panzer Division (*Hitlerjugend*) was believed to be up to its full strength of 21,000 men. The number of Panther tanks it had was undetermined. It was assumed that its operational role was north of Lisieux or east of the River Seine. However, in the event of an attack it was expected that it would be ready to operate south-east of 6th Airborne Division's drop and landing zones within twelve hours of the landings.

Generalleutnant Edgar **Feuchtinger 21 Panzer Division.**

21 Panzer Division was also believed to be up to full strength – 17,000 men – and had been stationed in Rennes until May when it was unexpectedly transferred to Caen. On the night of the 5/6 June 1944, the Division was actually on anti-invasion manoeuvres in the Caen area.

Panzer MkIVs of *21 Panzer Division* in Normandy.

Soldiers of the *Ost Bataillon* attached to *711 Infanterie Division* defending the area east of the River Orne. These were recruited from Russian prisoners of war. They would be in the best position to counter-attack the 6th Airborne Division.

In reaction to the invasion the Allies expected that the German forces would, after determining the strength of the landings and assuming they failed in an initial counter-attack, choose a line on the high ground east of the flooded valley of the River Dives and hold the invading forces there. Once the threat of the

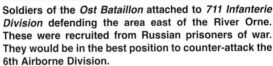

SS-*Standartenführer* Kurt Meyer (left) commanding *Panzergrenadier Regiment 25, 12 SS Panzerdivision (Hitlerjugend)* discusses unit dispositions with *Generalfeldmarschall* von Rundstedt prior to D-Day.

51

Ready to repel the greatest combined assault force in the history of warfare.

invasion had clearly declared itself west of the River Orne and there was no sign of an attack east of the River Dives or on the River Seine estuary, it was assumed that part of the *711 Infanterie Division* would move across to take up the high ground east of the River Dives, even though this would weaken the estuary defences on the River Seine. The reaction of the *716 Infanterie Division*, effectively in the middle of the invasion, was expected to be completely disrupted.

THE DECISION TO GO – D-DAY -1

The planned date for the invasion had been 5 June 1944, but low clouds, high winds and the bad conditions forecast by the meteorologists forced Eisenhower to postpone the invasion on the morning of 4 June. The weather front prevailed throughout the next day as predicted and Eisenhower feared the worst, for if the attack did not take place on 6 or 7 June there would be a wait of at least fourteen, possibly twenty-eight, days before the combination of moon, tide and time of sunrise would allow another attempt. Suspending the movement of over 2,000,000 men for this length of time without losing morale and letting the secret out seemed an impossible task. Also, if the invasion was to be rescheduled Rommel would be given even more time to prepare his growing defences. At 0330hrs on 5 June 1944, Eisenhower received some unexpected news.

Our little camp was shaking and shuddering under a wind of almost hurricane proportions and the accompanying rain seemed to be travelling in horizontal streaks. The mile long trip to the naval headquarters was anything but a cheerful one, since it seemed impossible that in such conditions there was any reason for even discussing the situation.

When the conference started the first report was given by Group Captain Stagg and the meteorological staff... Their astonishing declaration was that by the following morning a period of relatively good weather, heretofore completely unexpected, would ensue, lasting probably thirty-six hours...

The consequences of delay justified great risk and I quickly announced the decision to go ahead with the attack on June 6. The time was then 4.15 am, June 5.[5]

GENERAL DWIGHT 'IKE' EISENHOWER, SUPREME COMMANDER, ALLIED EXPEDITIONARY FORCE

The invasion fleet heads across the Channel to the Normandy coast.

As soon as the order had been given the wheels of the well-oiled Allied war machine were set in motion. The greatest combined assault force in the history of warfare was moving relentlessly towards its target on the French coastline of Normandy. At this point the potential outcome of the invasion was taken away from the politicians, chiefs of staff and planners, and transferred

Glider Pilots being briefed on the air corridors and flight paths.

to those soldiers, sailors and airmen who would have to endure the sharp end of war. In less than twenty-one hours the first British and Canadian paratroopers and gliderborne troops, of the 6th Airborne Division, would be fighting, and dying, on Normandy soil in the opening engagements for the battle for Normandy.

A loaded trailer is being pulled on to a Horsa.
Below: Photograph of the target area taken ten weeks before the assault (annotations added).

PEGASUS BR. 24 MAR '44 (VIEW LOOKING S.E.)

River Orne

LZ X

Caen Canal

Horsa and Hamilcar gliders ready to take off from Brize Norton towed by Halifax bombers.

Horsa glider in tow.

56

CHAPTER THREE

PEGASUS BRIDGE

THE FIRST ASSAULT

Pegasus Bridge (see Maps 1 & 2) is along the D514 between Caen and Ouistreham. Take the road to Bénouville and park your car near the *Café Gondrée* on west side of the Caen Canal before Pegasus Bridge. For more information on memorials and exhibits in this area refer to Ch. 6, A & B.

At 0016hrs, 6 June 1944, the first of the three Horsa gliders, chalk marked No. 91 and piloted by Staff Sergeant Jim Wallwork and Staff Sergeant Johnnie Ainsworth of the Glider Pilot Regiment, landed at LZ X. Aboard, leading the *coup de main* operation, was Company Commander Major John Howard, his wireless

The destination – Bénouville (Pegasus) Bridge and le Port on the left. To the right, Ranville (Horsa) Bridge. Note the white dots in many of the fields. These are 'Rommel's Asparagus', anti-glider poles. The 10ft-high timber poles were designed to rip apart any glider that tried to land in the area. They also provided an unwelcome hazard for descending paratroopers.

Cockpit of a Horsa glider during the fly-in

On their way – an Albemarle takes off with a Horsa in tow.

Superb flying skills put the gliders in exactly the right place.
Left: **Staff Sergeant Jimmy Wallwork.**

operator Corporal Ted Tappenden, Lieutenant Den Brotheridge and his twenty man strong assault troop from No. 25 Platoon of D Coy 2 Oxf Bucks. In addition, five sappers from No. 2 Platoon of 249 Fd Coy RE were on board to clear any explosives from the bridge.

Together with another five gliders, Major John Howard had a total of: thirty engineers, 132 assault troops, one HQ wireless operator, one officer and two NCOs from the RAMC, one officer from 7 Para and twelve glider pilots. These 180 men would form the first wave of Operation TONGA.

As a fine example of their extraordinary flying skills the men of the Glider Pilot Regiment put down their great wooden aircraft right on target at Bénouville Bridge. Later it was described by the Commander of the Allied Air Forces on D-Day, Air Vice-Marshal Leigh-Mallory, as *one of the most outstanding flying achievements of the war.* The sudden and violent impact rendered some of the men temporarily unconscious or disorientated, but the gliders had come to rest only 50 yards (47m) from their objective, now known as Pegasus Bridge.

Minutes later Brigadier Nigel Poett, CO of 5 Para Bde, came to ground on the east side of the River Orne near Ranville at DZ N (Map 1). After he had discarded his parachute harness he heard explosions and the distinctive crackle of Sten guns as Major Howard and his men stormed the bridge one mile (1.61km) or so east of his position. Brigadier Poett's first task was to gather his men and make his way to the troops fighting for Bénouville (Pegasus) Bridge over the Caen Canal and, 575 yards (525m) before, Ranville (Horsa) Bridge over the River Orne. The battle for Normandy had begun.

Walk over to the eastern side of Pegasus Bridge and position yourself, facing, due west, towards the *Café Gondrée*, at Point A (Map 2) on the Esplanade Major John Howard by the 50mm (1.97in) *KwK* (*Kampfwagenkanone*) anti-tank gun which is mounted in its Tobruk pit.

The night of 5/6 June 1944, had been warm, in keeping with the time of year, but the night sky was still unsettled after the storms of the previous day. Night vision, despite the full moon, varied because of high clouds and strong winds. At ground level though, the night air remained relatively still. *Schütze* Helmut Romer, a sixteen year old Berliner, together with another sentry, paced up and down the length of the bridge, their paths crossing every few minutes at the centre as they dutifully carried out their duties.[1]

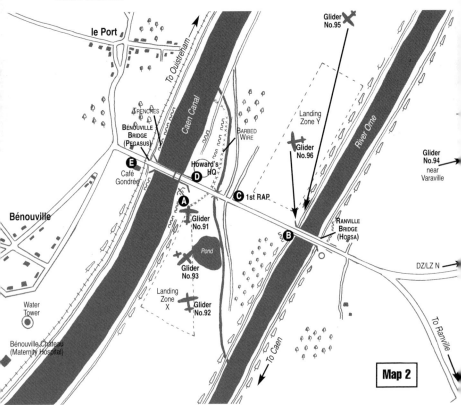

Across the road, due north, to your right, on the now flat piece of land and canal bank beyond the bridge, there once stood a pillbox with a machine-gun muzzle poking through its narrow slit. Nearer, still on your right, next to the bridge, was another pillbox which also doubled as the garrison HQ. To the left of this, along where the canal bank is now, the Germans were standing in their slit trenches. Those men of the fifty-strong garrison who were off duty, were asleep in their billets or had retired, having just changed the guard on the bridge, to Bénouville to enjoy the rest of their evening at the local brothel.[2]

The new Pegasus Bridge today seen from Point A Map 2.

The sky above Caen, some 5 miles (8.05km) away along the canal to your left, and along the Channel coastline, 3.5 miles (5.63km) to your right along the canal, was alight with searchlight beams and ack-ack fire as the Allied bombing raids softened up the German defences ready for the invasion. By the end of the night the war diaries of Bomber Command listed two new records. One for bombing missions flown in one night, 1,211 sorties and another for the greatest tonnage of bombs dropped in a single night, over 5,000 tons (5,080 tonnes). Their casualties amounted to only eight aircraft lost.[3]

The anti-tank gun was left unmanned on the night of the 5/6 June as the commander of the garrison, *Major* Hans Schmidt, did not have his men on full alert that evening. Adding to the Allies good fortune he had also failed to put the demolition charges into their chambers on the bridges in case they were accidentally set off or sabotaged by members of the French Resistance. Despite knowing the strategic importance of the bridges he protected, he had concluded that the stormy weather of the past few days would rule out an imminent invasion. After finishing his duty for the day *Major* Schmidt spent the night with his girlfriend in Ranville.[4]

Just after midnight on the night of the 5/6 June 1944 three

61

gliders descended into the area behind where you now stand. Unseen by the Germans and without making a sound, the pilots had swept the giant plywood birds through 180 degrees, reducing their airspeed from 160mph (257kmh) down to around 100mph (161kmh). They then deployed their arrester parachute brakes as they touched down on the small, 300 yard (274m) triangular LZ X, also known as EUSTON I, reducing their landing speed down to approximately 80mph (129kmh). The leading glider ploughed to a crashing halt at where now stands the first glider landing marker.

Just as ordered, the pilots had crushed the first defensive line of barbed wire around the bridge perimeter. Those guards who heard the crash dismissed the noise as the remnants of some striken Allied bomber falling to the ground. Had they been more alert, in the first half-minute or so while the crew and occupants of the glider were temporally dazed or even unconscious, the German machine-gunners could have slaughtered the British assault troop before they had even exited their aircraft.

The glider had lost its wheels on its first contact with the ground. The fuselage had bounced back into the air for a few seconds before landing again. The side door, which had already been opened during flight to help ensure a quick exit, gave the occupants a view of flashing sparks as the glider's metal skids struck the barbed wire fencing and stones on the ground. Those who witnessed the scene thought that they were under fire, believing the sparks were tracer bullets. So when glider No. 91 finally came to a standstill the troops were surprised when the sound of screeching metal, tearing canvas and splintering wood gave way only to silence.[5]

> The dazed silence did not seem to last long because we all came to our senses together on realising that there was no firing. There was no firing! It seemed quite unbelievable...
>
> Everyone automatically released their safety belts and felt their limbs for breakages. I realized that everything around me had gone very dark and my head

An RAF reconnaissance photograph taken on D-Day clearly shows how close the three gliders were to the bridge

was aching. My God I can't see! I clutched at my helmet and found that I must have hit the top of the glider during that last hell of a crash and all that had happened was that my battle bowler had come down over my eyes. What a relief! I quickly pushed it up and saw that the open door I was sitting in front of a few minutes earlier, because we had opened it in flight after we had cast off from the Halifax bombers, had completely

Major John Howard

disappeared. The door had collapsed because we had telescoped. The poor glider pilots were thrown right through the cockpit and over the wire. And we could hear them moaning, but we couldn't do anything about it because the great thing then, knowing where I'd got, first there, was to capture that bridge intact.

MAJOR JOHN HOWARD, COMPANY
COMMANDER, 2 OXF BUCKS

After the men had recovered from the initial shock of the landing and scrambled out from the wrecked hull of the glider, they instinctively carried out their assignments just as they had practised, time and time again, back in England on a swing bridge over the Exeter Canal. As No. 25 Platoon D Coy went into action Lieutenant Brotheridge sent Private Jack 'Bill' Bailey and two of his comrades to take out the pillbox containing the machine-gun. Within a minute of landing Major Howard saw his men storm the bridge just as the second glider, chalk marked No. 92 and piloted by Staff Sergeants Oliver Boland and Phillip Hobbs, crashed and came to a sudden stop before the pond.

The men of No. 24 Platoon D Coy, commanded by Lieutenant David Wood, quickly exited the glider and made their way to join the developing battle.

By this time Lieutenant Brotheridge had gathered his platoon and charged up the embankment on to the roadway over the bridge shouting their platoon call sign *Able, Able!* as they advanced; one of the bridge sentries, *Schütze* Romer, had just passed his opposite number and was heading for the east side when he was horrified to see the group of screaming, camouflaged, black-faced troops dashing towards him. The

Nearest two Horsa gliders with the *Café Gondrée* across the canal. The bridge structure can just be seen through the trees.

German soldier, with just a Mauser rifle for protection, took only seconds to assess the situation. He turned and fled, yelling, *Fallschirmjaeger!* (paratroopers) and dived into the nearest trench. The other sentry, an NCO, pulled out his flare pistol in order to raise the alarm.[6]

> *My job, as the bren gunner, was to rush the right-hand side of the bridge. Den Brotheridge got up and said, 'Come on, lads'. He ran. I followed him and as we made our approach to it I saw a German sentry with what looked like a Very light pistol in his hand. I fired and he went down, but at the same time he pulled the trigger of the Very pistol and the bright light went up. Still firing we went across.*
>
> PRIVATE BILL GRAY, 2 OXF BUCKS

The raiding party continued to execute their tasks. The Germans in their slit trenches and at their machine-gun posts, though stunned and shocked by the swift attack, soon became fully alert. Their own instincts for survival took over, causing the action to heat up.

> *I stopped and looked across the bridge just for a brief second. Looked at the Very light being shot up. Then I turned and one of the dugout doors half-opened and closed again. I shot across* [the

roadway]. *By this time I had a No. 36 grenade, the pin out. Into the dugout, opened and shut the door. The explosion went off. [Private] Charlie Gardner came in. I opened the door again and he just machine-gunned inside. Onto the second dugout and the same; in with the grenade, bang the door shut, explosion, smash it wide open again and Charlie finished them off. As we came back past the first dugout suddenly there was a moan or something from inside and I pulled out a 77 phosphorous. Took the cap off, gave it a twirl, undone the tape and jumped in and that went off.*

CORPORAL 'WALLY' PARR, 2 OXF BUCKS

Staff Sergeants Geoff Barkway and Peter Boyle had now landed the third glider, chalk marked No. 93, right on target, but perilously close to the pond. Again the glider passengers paid the price for the abrupt standstill of the glider.

I went shooting straight past those two pilots, through the whole bloody lot, shot out like a bullet and landed in front of the glider... I was covered in mud, I had lost my Sten gun and I didn't really know what I was bloody doing. Corporal Madge, one of my section commanders, brought me to my senses. He said, 'Well, what are you waiting for sir?'

LIEUTENANT RICHARD 'SANDY' SMITH,
2 OXF BUCKS

Lieutenant Smith pulled himself up out of the mud, picked up his Sten gun and made his way to the bridge. With him were other men from No. 14 Platoon B Coy who had been able to free themselves from the wreckage. On the ground, next to where Lieutenant Smith had been thrown, lay Captain John Vaughan, their medical officer. Having also been thrown out of the glider he was not so lucky and was left unconscious, face down, in the marshy ground. Half a dozen of the men had also been trapped in the wreckage and one of them, Bren gunner Lance Corporal Fred Greenhalgh, drowned in the pond. The time was 0018hrs. The first known British soldier had lost his life in Normandy on D-Day.

Lieutenant Richard Smith.

66

Major John Howard's glider, Pegasus Bridge is obscured by the trees

Taken from the same position today this photograph allows the new larger Pegasus Bridge to be seen more clearly

Sappers from No. 2 Platoon 249 Fd Coy RE had by this time scrambled across the superstructure of the bridge and begun looking for the explosives with the intention of hastily disconnecting and ripping out any fuse and detonation wires. As Brotheridge approached the eastern side he lobbed a grenade into the machine-gun nest on his right. Return fire, from the MG 34 or from a guard's *Schmeisser*, caught Brotheridge in the neck. He was thrown back by the force and lay sprawled in the middle of the road. Mortally wounded, he became the first acknowledged fatal casualty from enemy fire on D-Day (see Ch. 6, B8 & Ch. 7, B4). Private Bill Gray and the rest of the section proceeded with their tasks of systematically destroying the remaining machine-gun posts.

Feldwebel Heinz Hickman of the *Fallschirmjäger-Regiment 6*, accompanied by four men, had at this time just driven through le Port. He was about to make a left turn at the T junction at Bénouville in order to cross the bridge and continue his journey on to his HQ near Bréville, when he heard the distinctive rattle of the assault troops' Bren and Sten guns. He stopped the car, dismounted and split up his men into two patrols. They then continued cautiously to approach the bridge by edging down either side of the road as quickly as possible.

> *Then* [we saw them] *moving across the bridge. It was a full moon, very few clouds about. I recognised they were British soldiers. They can't be land forces so they must have come out of the air, either parachute or glider-borne troops. So* [we moved apart] *crept slowly forwards, I watched my blokes, said 'Come on, come on,' gave the order, 'don't start firing before I fire, wait for me.' I think we made more noise than we did hitting anybody so in the end we stayed there near the bridge, roughly about a hundred yards* [away] *firing, and I more or less ran out of ammunition....I'm not a coward but at that moment I got frightened. If you see a para platoon in full cry, they frighten the daylights out of you...the way they charge, the way they fire, the way they ran across the bridge....Then I gave the order to go back. What can I do with four men who had never been in action?*
>
> FELDWEBEL HEINZ HICKMAN, *FALLSCHIRMJÄGER-REGIMENT 6*

Lieutenant Smith was in the meantime hobbling across the catwalk – he had wrenched his knee in the landing – having received orders to take and secure the far side of the bridge. As he reached the end he gave a burst of fire from his Sten gun at a

German about to throw a stick grenade. He was too late. The grenade had already been primed and exploded as the bullet-ridden German fell dead on to the low wall in front of the cafe. The blast tore Smith's battle smock and trousers. Despite a deep laceration to the wrist on his trigger hand, he was still able to pull the trigger of his Sten and make his way forward towards the café. Leading his platoon they finished off the remaining resistance from the machine-gun pits and trenches. Later he was awarded the Military Cross for his bravery.

The east side of the bridge was thought to have been secured by No. 24 Platoon D Coy, and their commander, Lieutenant David Wood, decided to report the completion of his tasks to Major Howard. However, a German they had missed opened up with his *Schmeisser* and Wood took three bullets in his leg and fell to the ground in agony.

> *I was hit in the leg by a burst of fire, which also caught my platoon sergeant and my runner. I regret to say there were no heroics, although I had heard about folk who can run around on only one leg. I found I simply fell down and couldn't get up. My platoon medical orderly gave me a shot of morphia, applied a rifle splint and found my flask in my hip pocket.*
>
> LIEUTENANT DAVID WOOD, 2 OXF BUCKS

Corporal Claude Godbold temporarily took over command of No. 24 Platoon D Coy from Lieutenant Wood. By 0022hrs Major Howard had set up his command post in a trench at the pillbox on the north-east side of the bridge. As situation reports came in from his runners the results and cost of their assault became clearer. Captain Henry R.K. 'Jock' Neilson, commander of the sappers, was first to report to Major Howard with news that the bridge was clear of explosives. Then the bad news came. Three of his platoon commanders including his best friend, Den Brotheridge, had all been wounded. Corporal Wally Parr found Lieutenant Brotheridge's body.

Corporal 'Wally' Parr.

> *He was laying about 20 yards [18m] from the café in the middle of the road. I thought he was a German at first and then I stopped and*

69

Lieutenant Den Brotheridge, the first British soldier to be fatally wounded by enemy fire on D-Day.

realized, came back.... I put my hand under his head to lift him up. He just looked. His eyes sort of rolled back. He just choked and lay back. My hand was covered in blood... a terrible waste. The first thing that went through my mind. What a terrible waste.

CORPORAL WALLY PARR,
2 OXF BUCKS

As the firing dissipated Howard realized that his first objective, codename HAM, had been accomplished. The bridge over the canal was under their control. He then waited anxiously for news, via his radio operator Corporal Ted Tappenden, of the fate of No. 22 and No. 23 Platoons from D Coy, and No. 17 Platoon from B Coy. On board gliders chalk marked Nos. 94, 95 and 96, their objective was the bridge over the River Orne.

Pre-war photograph of the River Orne Bridge, looking east.

CHAPTER FOUR

HORSA BRIDGE

THE SECOND ASSAULT

From the anti-tank gun walk back to the road (D514) and head east towards Horsa Bridge. Just before the bridge on the left-hand side of the road is a memorial. The field directly behind the memorial is LZ Y, also known as EUSTON II, (see Maps 1 & 2) where glider chalk marked No. 96, containing No. 17 Platoon B Coy, led by Lieutenant Dennis Fox, landed 170 yards (155m) away at 0020hrs. Glider chalk marked No. 95, carrying Lieutenant 'Tod' Sweeney's No. 23 Platoon D Coy, dropped in an air pocket and came down, one minute later, some 700 yards (640m) short of the LZ. In glider chalk marked No. 94, due to a navigational error by the tug pilots, Staff Sergeants Lawrence and Shorter landed their glider east of Varaville at a bridge over the River Dives, leaving No. 22 Platoon D Coy, led by Lieutenant Charles Anthony 'Tony' Hooper, and Major Howard's 2ic, Captain Brian Priday, over 7 miles (11.27km) from their LZ (see Battleground Europe book *Merville Battery & The Dives Bridges* Ch. 8, A).

Walk towards the north-west corner of the bridge and look across the bridge. On 6 June 1944, the west side of the bridge had, for protection, two open machine-gun posts on the left side of the roadway and, on the right side, a camouflaged pillbox. Two obstacles, probably tree trunks, lay alongside the road to be used as road blocks if required.[1] Turn right and cross the road and position yourself facing west (looking back towards Pegasus Bridge) at Point B (Map 2 p.60). You now stand near where the sentry, at his machine-gun post, was, when Staff Sergeants Roy Howard and Freddie Baacke landed glider chalk marked No. 96 in the field (now obscured by the hedgerow and trees) just over 170 yards (155m) away to your right. This time there were no casualties when the glider landed and made a textbook stop.

> *'You're in the right place, Sir!' I shouted to Lieutenant Fox who seemed both happy and surprised at the same time as, with a drumming and crash of army boots along the floor of the glider, he disappeared into the night to shoot up the Germans guarding the bridge.*
>
> *It was up to Fred and me to unload the rest of the stores but now we received a shock as we climbed out through the door of the glider into the field. Where were the other gliders? We had been No. 96 and should have been the third glider to land in our field. Yet, apart from a herd of cows which had panicked in front of us as we landed, we were quite alone...alone in front of the*

Staff Sergeant Roy Howard.

whole invasion force which was not to land on the beaches 6 miles away until daybreak, and ahead of the main parachute drop by half an hour.
STAFF SERGEANT ROY HOWARD,
GLIDER PILOT REGIMENT.

Because of the noise coming from the canal bridge the German sentries were on full alert at their machine-gun posts. The British assault troops scrambled from their glider and then formed into their respective sections. Lieutenant Fox noticed that the corporal of his leading section was standing still, looking towards their objective. The corporal reported that he could see a machine gun by the bridge. Unperturbed, Lieutenant Fox decided to lead the troops to the bridge himself. He had only walked a few paces when the German sentry opened up with an MG 34. The burst of machine gun fire sent the men sprawling and diving for cover. Sergeant Charles 'Wagger' Thornton, though, had stayed behind in anticipation of enemy fire and immediately returned fire with his 2in (50.80mm) mortar.

Dear old Thornton had got from way back in his position a mortar going, and he put a mortar slap down, a fabulous shot right on the machine-gun, so we just rushed the bridge, all the chaps yelling, 'Fox, Fox, Fox, Fox'.
LIEUTENANT DENNIS FOX, 2 OXF BUCKS

The assault troops reached the bridge just in time to see the remaining German sentries running away from their posts. An NCO from the lead section jumped into their machine-gun post and turned the MG 34 on to the retreating guards. These were the only shots fired in the battle to capture the River Orne Bridge. The men spread out and again the sappers went to work removing detonation wires and searching for explosives. However, like the canal bridge, none had been put into their chambers and the explosives were later found at a house nearby that had been used by the Germans as a billet.

A minute after Fox's glider had landed, Staff Sergeants Stan

RAF reconnaissance photograph showing the glider next to Ranville (Horsa) Bridge.

Pearson and Len Guthrie landed glider chalk marked No. 95 just over half a mile (0.80km) away from the bridge. Lieutenant 'Tod' Sweeney assembled his men and set off, at the double, towards their objective. The only 'casualties' were those who never saw the drainage ditches and fell full length into the water. When the men finally reached the river bridge, Sweeney, sodden and soaked and leading from the front (he had been one of the first into a drainage ditch) was unnerved by the calm of the situation and the lack of opposition. Leaving one section on the west bank, he accompanied his two other sections on to the bridge.

> *I hadn't cottoned on to the fact that the bridge had been seized at all. As I was beginning to go across, I thought that someone was in fact there before me, but you still had that awful feeling as you went over the bridge that it might go up under your feet. I went racing across with my heart in my mouth, eventually coming to a halt, a bit disappointed... We were all worked up to kill the enemy, bayonet the enemy, be blown up or something.*
>
> LIEUTENANT HENRY 'TOD' SWEENEY, 2 OXF BUCKS

> *They got to the bridge and 'Tod' led his platoon, charging across it, not, of course, meeting any opposition. And there on the other side was nothing more than the unmistakable figure of Dennis Fox. Sweeney rushed up to him. 'Dennis, how are you? Is everything all right?'*
>
> *'Yes, I think so,' replied Dennis. 'But I can't find the bloody umpires!'[2]**
>
> CAPTAIN JOHN VAUGHAN,
> 224 PARA FD AMB RAMC, ATTACHED 2 OXF BUCKS

Back at the canal bridge at approximately 0026hrs Major Howard had finally received the message he had been waiting for: Lieutenant Sweeney reported that the bridge over the River Orne had been captured intact. Howard was exhilarated by the news. They had

* The *coup de main* operation had been rehearsed many times, under the watchful eye of military umpires, on two similarly positioned bridges on the outskirts of Exeter back in England. It was the ease in which they took their real objective, after all the arduous training, which prompted Lt Fox's ironic response. The Countess Wear Bridge, over the River Exe, and the swing bridge over the Exeter Canal are still there today. In 1994 a plaque was unveiled next to the swing bridge acknowledging their use in the operation.

captured both bridges in only ten minutes! He immediately ordered Sweeney to secure the bridge and to send Fox's platoon over to join the others at the canal bridge in anticipation of a counter-attack from Bénouville. Finally, Howard told Corporal Tappenden to send out the two prearranged code words on his wireless set to notify 5 Para Bde HQ and their relieving force, 7 Para, of his troop's success. HAM and JAM was transmitted ceaselessly over the airwaves in the direction of DZ N near Ranville.

Later, back at the east side of the river bridge where there was a small, lone, country house, Sweeney greeted the old couple who lived there and explained to

The River Orne Bridge with the German sign still in position.

Lieutenant Henry 'Tod' Sweeney.

them why his men were there; *Pour la liberation de la France.* But four years of Nazi occupancy couldn't be forgotten so quickly. Suspecting a German ruse and ever fearful of a visit by the Gestapo the elderly couple kept themselves to themselves. When the little old lady realized what had really happened later that day she made amends by greeting Sweeney with a kiss.[3]

Sometime after capturing the river bridge the sound of a patrol was heard approaching from the tow path, on the east side of the river, from the direction of Caen.

> *They were challenged by the section on that side of the road. They shouted back something that sounded German, so the section opened fire and killed them all. We found them there the next morning. Unfortunately, one of the people in that bunch was a [British] paratrooper.*
>
> LIEUTENANT HENRY 'TOD' SWEENEY, 2 OXF BUCKS

The paratrooper, gagged by his captors, turned out to be a pathfinder from the 22 (Ind) Para Coy. He had been captured by a patrol from *21 Panzer Division*, who were on anti-invasion manoeuvres in that area, and was evidently being taken back to their headquarters for interrogation.[4]

By this time the German garrison commander of the bridges had been alerted to the disturbance at the bridges and had set off, in haste, from Ranville to investigate the trouble. On the east side of the River Orne Bridge Lieutenant Sweeney's men were alerted again to a sound approaching the bridge.

> *We heard the grinding of gears and the noise of what sounded like a very heavy vehicle coming round the corner... I thought, 'Well, here we go. This is the first tank attack'. And I got everybody ready. Around the corner came low dimmed yellow lights and the grinding of gears with the sound of a track running. So I sent a message over the air. Down the road came an open half-track – an officer's vehicle – followed by a motorcyclist. We were all down in the ditches on the side of the road so we were looking up and as it passed everyone opened fire.*
>
> LIEUTENANT HENRY 'TOD' SWEENEY, 2 OXF BUCKS

Hitting, but not stopping, the vehicle, the troops on the east side of the bridge had more luck with the motorcycle. The Bren gunner killed the driver, causing the motorcycle to fly off the roadway and into the river. The staff car, however, carried on across the bridge. Sweeney, who at this time, was with his guard section on the west bank, opened up with his Sten gun. The driver, hit and badly wounded, lost control. The vehicle careered into a ditch. Sweeney's men surrounded the car and dragged out the occupants. Among the wreckage the men found empty wine bottles, dirty plates, face-powder, rouge, stockings and lingerie![5] *Major* Hans Schmidt had returned to his post. Lieutenant Sweeney had the wounded Germans put on stretchers and transferred to the temporary Regimental Aid Post (RAP). This had been set up by Major Howard, some 150 yards (137m) down the road, towards Pegasus Bridge.

From where you now stand follow the road west back towards Pegasus Bridge. This is the same route along which Sweeney's men carried the Germans to the RAP. At the small lane to your right, some 410 yards (375m) from Pegasus Bridge stop (at what is now a roundabout) Point C (Map 2). It was near here in a ditch and along a bank that the wounded were brought and tended to by the medical orderlies and their medical officer, Captain John Vaughan. By 0700hrs Captain Vaughan would have several dead and fifteen wounded personnel at his RAP.

Captain Vaughan had soon regained consciousness as the battle raged for the capture of Pegasus Bridge. His first concern had been to help a man still trapped in the wrecked glider hull. Unable to free him, he had given him a shot of morphia from a syrette and reassured him that he would find a stretcher-bearer. He then staggered off in search of his medical orderlies. On his way Captain Vaughan met his medical corporal – who had been sent by Major Howard to find him – as he stumbled into the roadway between the two bridges. A few minutes later, after a swig from Major Howard's whisky flask, Captain Vaughan set off to find and treat his casualties.

Captain John Vaughan.

I found Den [Brotheridge] *lying near a low stone wall at the west end of the café. He was looking at the stars, bewilderment on his face and a bullet hole in the middle of his neck below the chin... All I could do was give him a shot of morphia. By then I had got some*

77

*medical orderlies together and we carried him back to the RAP...
David Wood I found near the anti-tank gun pit, his thigh
shattered by machine-gun bullets. He had no thought for himself
but kept on asking how Den was getting on.*

Captain John Vaughan,
224 Para Fd Amb RAMC, attached to 2 Oxf Bucks

Twenty-six year old Lieutenant Brotheridge died shortly
thereafter. *Major* Hans Schmidt, by the time he reached the RAP,
had recovered from the initial shock of being wounded and
captured. He harassed Captain Vaughan while his wounds were
being treated.

*He harangued me about the futility of this Allied attempt to
defeat the master race. We were undoubtedly going to end up in
the sea he assured me with complete conviction... He ended his
lecture by requesting me to shoot him. This I did – in the bottom
– with a needle attached to a syringe of morphia. The effect of
this, it seemed, induced him to take a more reasonable view of
things and in about ten minutes he actually thanked me for my
medical attentions.*

Captain John Vaughan,
224 Para Fd Amb RAMC, attached to 2 Oxf Bucks

He was unable to help Schmidt's sixteen year old driver though.
Without the use of proper medical instruments or supplies,
Captain Vaughan amputated one of the driver's legs with a pair
of scissors, the bone having been already shattered by the impact
of the bullets. But with no blood to carry out a transfusion the
young German died within half an hour. From this point
onwards Captain Vaughan and the medical orderlies were kept
busy.

The commander of *Panzerjäger Abteilung 716* of *716 Infanterie
Divison*, equipped with mobile *Hotchkiss 7.5cm (2.95in) Pak 40s*
on tracked chassis, had already prepared the first of their
counter-attacks on Pegasus Bridge.

CHAPTER FIVE

COUNTER-ATTACK AND REINFORCEMENTS

HOLDING UNTIL RELIEVED

Walk east along the D514, back towards Pegasus Bridge, and to the open area of land by the side of the canal on your right-hand side; this is where Major John Howard set up his command post, in a trench, in front of a German pillbox. Stop at Point D (Map 2 p.60).

At 0050hrs, precisely as planned, Major Howard heard the distinctive heavy rumble of approaching aircraft. Flying at less than 500ft (152m) an armada of Dakotas, Stirlings and Albemarles was making its way to DZ N in order to drop the men of 5 Para Bde. This area, situated in the cornfields north of Ranville, had been marked by the pathfinders of 22 (Ind) Para Coy with ground flares to aid the navigators and pilots of the RAF. With the arrival of this force Major Howard expected the

An armada of Horsa gliders towed by Stirlings making its way to the drop zone.

first troops from 7 Para to arrive very soon and help reinforce his tenuous position – but it was not to be. High winds, reduced visibility and a variety of other factors meant that the 2,200 paratroopers of the three battalions had been spread over a far wider area than had been anticipated. The first large group of reinforcements did not arrive at Pegasus Bridge for another fifty minutes and then, when they did, they were only at one-third strength and missing much of their heavy equipment. It was this loss of mortars, wireless sets and medium machine-guns that would hinder their progress in the hours to come.

Brigadier Nigel Poett.

German anti-aircraft activity in the area east of the River Orne increased as the 262 Allied aircraft made their way over the DZs and LZs of K,N and V (Map 1, p.26). The night sky was lit up by the searchlight beams and the blue-green tracer fire from the German ground defences. As the canopies of silk began to blossom beneath the aircraft Major Howard, a former policeman, blew on his old police whistle the pre-arranged V for Victory signal; this sound would inform any paratroopers who heard it that the bridges had been taken intact. Furthermore, it was hoped, the sound would help them find their orientation.

At 0052hrs Brigadier Nigel Poett, commander of 5 Para Bde who had dropped with the pathfinders, arrived at the River Orne Bridge accompanied only by a private. He had never received Corporal Tappenden's wireless call as his own operator, Lieutenant Gordon Royle, had been killed when he attacked an enemy patrol single-handed at the DZ. Nevertheless Brigadier Poett continued on towards Major Howard's Headquarters and arrived just in time to witness the Germans' first counter-attack.

When I reached Howard, stronger efforts were already being made by the Germans to regain the bridges. One of these included a tank. The tank was most effectively dealt with by a PIAT [an infantry anti-tank weapon firing a powerful bomb]. *It was a short-range weapon and complicated to reload. It was,*

80

therefore, essentially a one shot weapon in action, requiring a cool head and steady hand, plus a great deal of courage in facing a tank at close range. Howard's Sergeant Thornton had all these qualities.

Brigadier Nigel Poett, Commander, 5 Para Bde.

Continue to walk over Pegasus Bridge and stop by the road outside the entrance of the *Café Gondrée* at Point E (Map 2 p.60). From this vantage point Howard's defences can be easily imagined. Back at his command post Howard kept Lieutenant Wood's No. 24 Platoon of D Coy, and the sappers in reserve on the east side of Pegasus Bridge. The grounds of the *Café Gondrée* were held by Lieutenant Brotheridge's No. 25 Platoon of D Coy and Lieutenant Smith – who had now also taken command of Brotheridge's platoon, had his own No. 14 Platoon of B Coy, in the bunkers and trenches across the road. Up ahead, towards the T junction (now a roundabout), Lieutenant Fox's No. 17 Platoon of B Coy, waited anxiously for the expected counter-attack.

By 0115hrs, Major Howard had secured his defences as best he could with the relatively small number of men under his command. At 0130hrs his troops were put to the test as the sound of armoured vehicles was heard approaching from the direction of Bénouville towards the T junction just 350 yards (320m) up the road.

The clanking and grinding of the caterpillar tracks became louder as the German armour turned on to the roadway leading to the bridge. The sense of danger was heightened due to the lack of suitable ammunition; the No. 82 (gammon) grenades – ideal for use against tank and armoured vehicle tracks – couldn't be found and most of the PIATs had been damaged and rendered useless due to the severity of the gliders' crash-landings. Only one serviceable PIAT was found and the responsibility of firing this fell on Sergeant 'Wagger' Thornton, of Lieutenant Fox's Platoon, who was positioned nearest the T junction.

Although he had two PIAT bombs, Thornton knew that if he missed with the first shot he would not have a chance to reload the cumbersome weapon before the armoured vehicle returned fire. As the vehicles drew closer the men held their fire and paused, with baited breath, in anticipation of the outcome. Thornton, alone in his task, waited nervously for his target to come into range of his first, and only, shot.

I don't mind admitting it I was shaking like a bloody leaf as this bloody great thing appears. The lads behind me were only lightly armed with Bren guns, rifles and grenades. They wouldn't stand a chance if I missed and the whole operation would be over. I was so nervous I was talking to myself, 'This is it! You mustn't miss.' The first tank had begun moving slowly down the road. I pulled the trigger on the PIAT. It was a direct hit. Machine-gun clips inside the tank set off grenades which set off shells. There was the most enormous explosion, with bits and pieces flying everywhere and lighting up the darkness. To my delight, the other tank fled... I was so excited and so shaking I had to move back a bit.

SERGEANT 'WAGGER' THORNTON, 2 OXF BUCKS

The spectacular display lasted for nearly half an hour and in doing so blocked the path of the following tanks. It was enough to convince the Germans that the British were holding the bridge in strength and so they decided to wait until dawn before they would counter-attack again. This gave the men of 2 Oxf Bucks a much needed breathing space until their reinforcements arrived.

Lieutenant Colonel Richard Geoffrey Pine-Coffin.

At the same time as the armoured column arrived at Bénouville, just over a mile (1.6km) away on DZ N, Lieutenant Colonel Richard Geoffrey Pine-Coffin, Commander of 7 Para, could hear the sound of Major Howard's whistle relaying the success signal at 0130hrs. At this time he also had less than fifty per cent of his riflemen and Bren gunners assembled at the RV. Worse still he had no medium machine-guns, mortars or wireless sets. Nevertheless, he decided he could wait no longer and set off for the bridges.

82

I set off with my initial attack force [A B C Coys and the Adv Bn HQ]. *The plan was for rear Bn HQ to follow up in its own best time, so I left the 2ic* [Steele-Baume] *to collect in all he could and follow us up, choosing his own time for starting…. As the bridges were intact I took my force over them with all speed and ordered them into their prearranged bridgehead positions in Bénouville… It was 0140hrs when I crossed the canal bridge with this force.*

LIEUTENANT COLONEL RICHARD GEOFFREY PINE-COFFIN, CO 7 PARA

On their arrival they passed through 2 Oxf Bucks positions and split up into three companies. A Coy of 7 Para went down the canal path and set up their defences around the houses in the southern part of Bénouville. B Coy of 7 Para went off to the right of the bridge and set up a defence perimeter in le Port and nearby woods; meanwhile C Coy of 7 Para worked their way towards the grounds of the château which was being used as a

German self-propelled *Hotchkiss 7.5cm Pak 40(SF) auf GW 39 H (f)*. Similar to vehicle knocked out by Sergeant 'Wagger' Thornton.

The road leading from Pegasus Bridge to the 'T' junction between Bénouville and le Port

maternity hospital. 7 Para had barely 200 men between the three companies and, even though some stragglers did join the battalion later, this depleted force suffered severe casualties fighting off the numerous German counter-attacks around the village of Bénouville. In less than two and a half hours of dropping into Normandy, 7 Para had sustained terrible casualties in their initial battle against German forces. The brief war diary entry of 7 Para, for 0325hrs on 6 June, graphically demonstrates their situation:

> *Place: le Port and Bénouville. 0325[hrs] Bn occupied objective and held it against various counter-attacks. A and B Coys being heavily engaged. Cas[ualties] killed 3 officers, Capt Parry (Padre), Lt Bowyer and Lt Hill, and 16 Ors. Wounded 4 officers, Major Taylor, Capt Webber, Lt Hunter & Lt Temple & 38 Ors. Missing 170 Ors did not RV after drop.*
>
> WAR DIARY 7 PARA

At one point A Coy was cut off and by daybreak they had lost all of their officers. B Coy were under constant sniper fire in le Port, some of the snipers being in the church tower. Corporal Tommy Killeen dealt with this by blowing a hole in the church tower with a PIAT round. Later the corporal was seen removing his helmet in respect before he entered the church![1] Some twelve bodies of German snipers were found in the wrecked church tower.

84

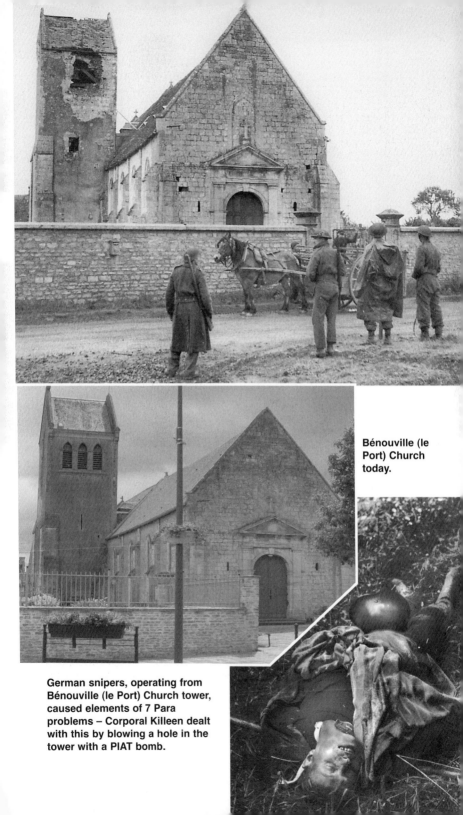

Bénouville (le Port) Church today.

German snipers, operating from Bénouville (le Port) Church tower, caused elements of 7 Para problems – Corporal Killeen dealt with this by blowing a hole in the tower with a PIAT bomb.

One German counter-attack, using tanks as support, was repulsed largely due to the efforts of Private Michael McGee, who single-handedly put one of the tanks out of action by running up to it and placing a gammon bomb onto its tracks. For his action he was awarded the DCM.

The Germans that advanced into Bénouville were from the *21 Panzer Division*. Among them was *Panzergrenadier Regiment 192*. One of the officers was *Leutnant* Hans Höller, his section of mobile *75mm* (2.95in) *Pak 40s*, were hidden in the hedgerows about 300 yards (274m) from the château.

We got involved in heavy fighting with a strong parachute unit. We managed to penetrate into half the village, but the parachutists fought bitterly and the exit leading to the coast could not be taken.

LEUTNANT HANS HÖLLER,
PZGREN REGT 192

Leutnant Hans Höller on D-Day.

C Coy were also threatened by the German armour; they were preparing for trouble as a number of German tanks approached their positions in the château grounds when, to everyone's amazement, the tanks stopped and the crews dismounted and assembled in front of the lead tank for a discussion. Wasting no time, C Coy opened fire on the surprised Germans. Those who survived immediately drove their tanks away from the bridge, heading for the coast. During the fighting the Germans had occupied part of the château, but were eventually driven out by the paratroopers. Although the château was in the middle of the battlefield throughout the month of June, the matron, Madame Vion, continued to run the hospital with efficiency and delivered eighteen babies during the first eight weeks of the invasion.

During the fighting Georges and Thérèse Gondrée, with their two children, had been taking shelter in the *Café Gondrée* cellar. Georges answered a knock at his door and invited in two armed soldiers in battledress. After a brief exchange of words he took the soldiers to meet his family and soon realized that this was

A German Marder III self-propelled gun passing a crashed Horsa glider.

not a German trick but that the invasion had really started. Later Georges Gondrée suggested that the café should be used for the wounded. This offer was taken up when at 0920hrs Captain Urquhart, from 225 Para Fd Amb, established a Regimental Aid Post (RAP) at the Café for 7 Para and 2 Oxf Bucks casualties. To show his appreciation to the Allied troops, Georges Gondrée went into his garden and dug up ninety-eight bottles of champagne that he had buried back in 1940 when the Germans had occupied the country. It was a gesture that turned into a tradition and the Gondrée family have continued to show their gratitude ever since, as no D-Day veteran has ever had to buy a drink in the *Café Gondrée*.

As H-Hour approached for the seaborne landings a rumbling crescendo of noise from the naval bombardment nearly

Leutnant **Hans Höller and his 75mm anti-tank gun hidden in the hedgerow near** *Bénouville Château.*

Italian prisoners who, when released, returned to their task of putting up anti-glider poles – much to the amusement of their captors.

drowned out the noise of small arms and mortar fire around the bridge. It was at this time that two Italian prisoners were brought in. It turned out that they were labourers being used to erect the anti-glider poles in the fields around the bridges and Ranville. After some questioning, Major Howard turned them loose and to his surprise they returned to their work in the field. When questioned further, they confessed that they had specific orders to have the poles in position by the end of 6 June. Convinced that the Germans would return, they were more afraid of the consequences of not carrying out their orders than

Major General Gale at his HQ at Ranville talking to war correspondent Leonard Moseley (far right) who had jumped with the 6th Airborne.

they were of trying to work in a battlefield. So, and to everyone's amusement, they were left to get on with erecting the poles around the crashed gliders.[2]

At around 0900hrs forty-seven year old Major General Richard Gale, accompanied by Brigadier The Hon Hugh Kindersley and Brigadier Nigel Poett, left his HQ in Ranville to discuss with Lieutenant Colonel Pine-Coffin the situation in Bénouville and le Port. Just as he arrived at Pegasus Bridge two German gunboats were seen approaching the bridge from the direction of Ouistreham. The lead boat began firing its 20mm (0.79in) gun at the bridge. 7 Para on the west bank opened fire and at the same time Private Claude Godbold, 2 Oxf Bucks, fired a PIAT bomb which exploded in the wheelhouse. Out of control, the boat ran into the east bank. The other gunboat turned around

German gunboat crippled by a PIAT bomb launched by Private Godbold, 2 Oxf Bucks.

and headed back to the coast.[3]

Later the Germans tried to destroy the bridge by sending a *Focke-Wulf FW190* fighter bomber. The pilot scored a direct hit on top of the bridge, but the single bomb never detonated and bounced off the bridge and into the water, leaving only a big dent on top of the bridge counter-weight. Two German frogmen were also sent down the canal to lay charges on the bridge, but these were seen and disposed of by British snipers.

THE AIRBORNE AND SEABORNE LINK-UP

At 1230hrs[4] the men at the bridge heard the unmistakable sound of bagpipes approaching from the direction of Ouistreham. Soon the sight of Piper Bill Millin playing his pipes and Brigadier The Lord Lovat wearing his green beret and carrying a walking stick, came into view. With them there was a Churchill tank and the commandos of 1 SS Bde.

Piper Bill Millin, 1 SS Bde.

Piper Bill Millin with his bagpipes at the 65th Anniversary. The bagpipes are now on display at the Pegasus Memorial Museum.

> *I stopped piping immediately across the road from the café. There was a battle going on. There were huge columns of black smoke and even from where I was standing I could hear shrapnel and bullets or whatever hitting off the metal side of the bridge. Wounded were being carried up from the canal banks and then to the café. It was a real hot spot. Lovat went forward to speak with Major Howard and he said, 'John, today we are making history.' Lovat came back to me and said 'Right, we'll cross over. Now, don't play, wait until I tell you.' So we walked over ducking because of the snipers. We almost got to the other side and he said, 'Right play now and keep playing all the way along this road until you come to another bridge and keep playing right across – no matter what just keep playing.'*
>
> PIPER BILL MILLIN, 1 SS BDE

Not all the commandos were lucky in crossing Pegasus Bridge and several of them were killed by

snipers. Captain John Vaughan saw one drop right in front of him. He had been shot in the head through his green beret. Commandos who crossed the bridge later chose to wear their steel helmets. The ground between the bridges offered some relief from the snipers as the trees along the canal bank blocked their field of view. But crossing the next bridge they were once again in the open.

> *I looked across and I could see two airborne on the other side dug in a slit trench. I kept my eye on those two chaps. They were signalling, 'down, down,' and pointing to the sides of the river. They kept looking at Lovat. He was walking along there as if he was out for a walk on his estate... It was the longest bridge I walked over. But anyway, I piped over that, playing the 'Blue Bonnets Over the Border'. The two airborne chaps thought we were crazy because we hadn't taken any notice. But I got over, stopped playing the pipes and shook hands with the two chaps in their slit trench. Then from across the road appears this tall airborne officer, red beret on. He came marching across, his arms outstretched towards Lovat; 'Very pleased to see you, old boy,' and Lovat said, 'And we are very pleased to see you, old boy. Sorry we are two and a half minutes late!' We were more than two and a half minutes late but that's the famous words of the link-up of the airborne and commandos.*
>
> PIPER BILL MILLIN, NO 1 SS BDE

The commandos then advanced towards the high ground around Amfréville to help the men of 3 Para Bde hold a defensive perimeter east of the River Orne. As the afternoon passed by more reinforcements arrived from the beaches. By the evening 3rd Infantry Division, whose main objective was forming the link-up between the airborne and seaborne troops and pushing on towards Caen, had established and were holding a bridgehead 5 miles (8.05km) deep and 4 miles (2.39km) wide between the Caen Canal and Ver-sur-Mer. All that separated British 3rd Infantry Division from the Canadian 3rd Infantry Division, who had landed on JUNO Beach, was the village of Langrune-sur-Mer. This was still being fought for by the troops of No. 48 Royal Marine Commando (48 RM Cdo), a fight that would continue throughout the night of the 6 June. To the east 2 Warwicks, had passed through St Aubin and Bénouville and were dug in around Blainville, while 1 KOSB took up positions in St Aubin which overlooked Bénouville. As they did so, the engineers from 17 Fd Coy moved up and began the task of building relief Bailey bridges across the canal.[5]

At 2100hrs, as dusk started to settle over the Normandy battlefields, the troops on both sides were greeted with a spectacular display that had never before been witnessed on such a scale in the history of warfare. An air armada of aircraft pulling 244 gliders was heading for the LZ/DZs of N & W. On board over 3,000 troops with supplies and heavy equipment were waiting to reinforce the 6th Airborne Division bridgehead.

Among the reinforcements were 6 Airldg Bde HQ, 1 RUR, 6 AARR, A Coy 12 Devons, 716 Ab Lt Comp Coy RASC, 249 Fd Coy RE, 211 Airldg Lt Bty, two companies of 195 Airldg Fd Amb and the remainder of 2 Oxf Bucks. The landings proved to be a truly memorable experience, particularly for those on board the gliders:

> *There were just the three of us and we carried, in the glider, a 6-pounder [2.72kg) anti-tank gun and a jeep... When we landed there were several bangs, as we ran over stuff on the ground. The cockpit door was open, and I could see we were approaching a tall hedge at speed. However, we went straight through it and didn't feel a thing. We finally came to a stop in the corner of a field near Bénouville and immediately removed the tail of the glider. I started to unshackle the gun and jeep and suddenly realized that I was on my own. I looked all around and couldn't see a soul. I called out and first one head, then another, appeared in the long grass at the side of the field. One of them said they had seen tanks. So I started up the jeep and drove the jeep and gun straight out of the glider without bothering to put down the ramps. Unfortunately I hadn't taken out the blocks from the springs of the jeep, which were used to make it solid for lashing down, so I got quite a jolt when it hit the ground. I suppose it was a drop of about 5 feet [1.52m]. As it happened, the tanks were Shermans, so no panic.*

Private Don Mason, 2 Oxf Bucks.

PRIVATE DON MASON, 2 OXF BUCKS

On landing the men assembled and moved off towards Bénouville as quickly as possible. As the other companies of 2 Oxf Bucks joined their comrades of B and D Coys at the bridge they received a lot of jovial comments about their late arrival. 2

Hamilcar gliders landing on DZ/LZ N at 2100hrs on D-Day.

Oxf Bucks, including Major Howard's company, then moved into Ranville that evening to prepare for their attack on Escoville the following day.

The Germans however, were still well within range of the landing zones and they were constantly firing at the gliders that came into land.

> *The flight over the channel was uneventful, but things started to hot up once we crossed the Normandy coastline... On touchdown, our undercarriage was ripped away but we completed the fast bumpy landing on skids. All aboard got out of the craft as quickly as possible. On setting foot on Normandy soil I was aware the Germans were using automatic fire, some of which punctured the fuselage of our glider. It was at this time I saw the body of Private Leonard Worgan lying on the grass. He had been killed in the glider by German tracer fire. Being in daylight view of the enemy and under constant fire, it was decided to get away fast from the landing field.*
> PRIVATE RAYMOND DAECHE, 195 AIRLDG FD AMB RAMC

Private Leonard Worgan was later buried in Ranville churchyard, where he still rests today, near the grave of Lieutenant Den Brotheridge. After their landing 195 Airldg Fd Amb RAMC made its way over the bridges to set up a Main Dressing Station (MDS) in a house in Ranville near the château being used by 225 Para Fd Amb RAMC as their MDS.

Meanwhile at the RAP in the *Café Gondrée*, one soldier from 7 Para, witnessed the landings while he was sitting at a table just outside the front door of the Café, waiting for his turn to be tended in the aid post.

> *Georges Gondrée brought me a glass of champagne, which was very welcome indeed after that sort of day, I can tell you... Just*

Reinforcements crossing Pegasus Bridge.

Private Gardner (glider No. 91), Captain B. Priday (with Sten gun) and Lance Corporal Lambley (glider No. 94). Only Captain Priday survived the war.

before it got dark, there was a tremendous flight of aircraft, hundreds of British aircraft. They came in and they did a glider drop and a supply drop between the bridges and the coast on our side of the canal. It was a marvellous sight, it really was. They were also dropping supplies on the 'chutes out of their bomb doors, and then it seemed only a few minutes afterwards that all these chaps in jeeps, towing anti-tank guns and god knows what, were coming down the road through le Port, and over this bridge. At that moment I can remember thinking to myself, 'My God, we've done it!

MAJOR NIGEL TAYLOR, 7 PARA

As the men dug in for the night the Germans were already setting up their defences and preparing their counter-attacks. *21 Panzer Division* were in place between 3rd Infantry Division and around Caen and *12 SS Panzer Division Hitlerjugend* were already forward. In the days to come the Allied infantry, paratroopers and commandos found that these élite units were to be more difficult to contend with than the coastal defence infantry of *716 Infanterie Division*.

Soldiers of *12 SS Panzer Division Hitlerjugend* . This élite unit along with *21 Panzer Division* were about to give 6th Airborne a hard fight.

CHAPTER SIX

Memorial Tour of Battlefield No. 1

Pegasus Bridge – Horsa Bridge

Distance between stops by vehicle: 0.2 miles (0.32km)
Total walking distance at stops: Approx 3 miles (4.83km)
Recommended time allowed for tour: 2 to 3 hours

For convenience the tour is best started at Pegasus Bridge, first and foremost because this was the scene of the first battle on that morning. It is also the most well known, and today most easily found, of the objectives that 6th Airborne Division were tasked with taking on D-Day. An added benefit to starting here is the famous *Café Gondrée*. When you arrive it would be a good idea to have a drink in the comfortable surroundings of Madame Gondrée-Pritchett's terrace café. Spend a few minutes reading the following section to familiarize yourself with the immediate area and then begin your tour. A look inside the café, at the memorabilia, weapons and uniforms, will also help give you a clearer picture of what life was like for the airborne soldiers as they embarked upon their mission of liberation.

Madame Arlette Gondrée-Pritchett outside the Café Gondrée.

If your arrival in France is by ferry at Ouistreham then Pegasus Bridge can be found by taking the D514 to Bénouville. Alternatively, if you are approaching from Caen, take the D515 (signposted for Ouistreham car ferry) until you see the sign for Bénouville on the D514. Take this road, go straight on at the roundabout and you will see the new Pegasus Bridge in front of you. Park in the car park on the right-hand side, just before the *Café Gondrée*, and walk around to the front of the café and stop just before you reach the bridge (for a more detailed explanation of the battle and tour of the battlefield, refer to Chs. 2, 3 & 4).

97

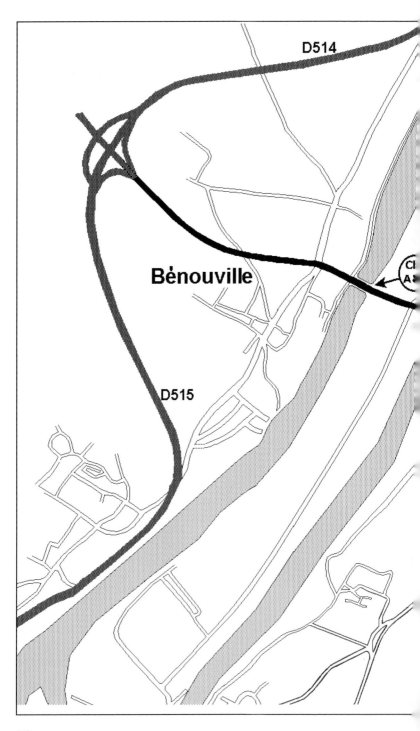

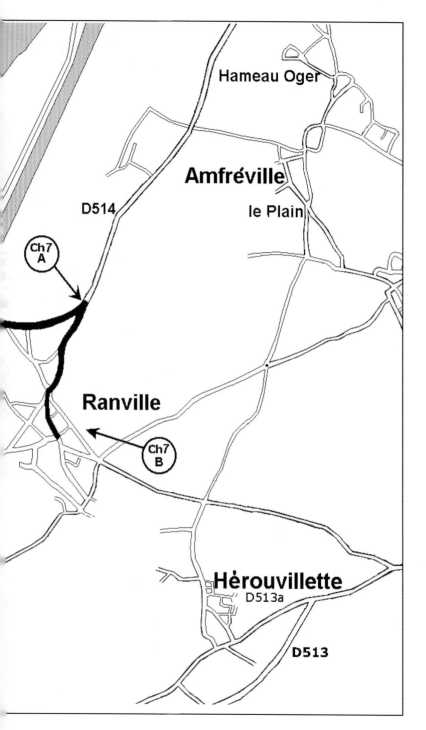

A. Pegasus Bridge & Horsa Bridge

To the right of Pegasus Bridge is:

1) *Pegasus Bridge signpost*. This bears the now famous emblem and name. This sign was presented to the inhabitants of Bénouville in June 2003 by the Gloucestershire branch of the Parachute Regiment Association. This replaces the sign renovated by the Airborne Assault Normandy Trust in 1996, which is now situated in the Memorial Pegasus Park (see Ch. 6, B11). The original sign was designed and made in the workshops of 286 Fd Pk Coy RE here in June 1944. The idea for the sign came about after the arrival in France of the 51st Highland Division who had been nicknamed the 'Highway Decorators' for their habit of daubing their insignia HD on the walls of any place they had fought. Lieutenant Colonel Frank Lowman decided to seek the permission of Major General Gale for his men to build and erect their own insignia sign by the canal bridge. Permission was granted and two signs were erected. The second sign stands at the opposite end of the bridge near the lane leading to the Memorial Pegasus Museum (an original sign is in the museum). These signs were officially unveiled in front of local dignitaries on 26 June 1944.

The original Pegasus Bridge was replaced in the winter of 1993, six months before the fiftieth anniversary of the D-Day landings. Many thought, not least the veterans and locals, that the decision to replace the bridge at that particular time was both insensitive and thoughtless. But the powers-that-be felt that the work – to widen the Caen Canal so that larger ships could reach the Port of Caen – could not wait. When one eighty year old veteran crossed the original bridge for the last time he graciously conceded:

> *My biggest thought walking across the bridge today is this is the last time. But they need a new bridge and that's that. We can't stop progress.*
>
> MAJOR JOHN HOWARD, 2 OXF BUCKS

The original Pegasus Bridge now forms the centrepiece to the Memorial Pegasus Museum Park (See Ch. 6, B24). Pegasus Bridge gains its name in honour of the British 6th Airborne Division, and the name and sign was adopted from the divisional flash of the British airborne forces in the 1940s. Chosen by Lieutenant General Sir Frederick 'Boy' Browning in

1941, when he was appointed to raise the airborne forces, the flash was later designed, in May 1942, by Major Edward Seago. The flash was to be worn on the upper arm of all airborne troops. Sadly, the distinctive flash was withdrawn from the airborne forces on 1 September 1999, after a reorganisation of the British armed forces in a strategic defence review in which 16 Air Assault Brigade was formed. This was contrary to the feelings of most veterans and serving troops of The Parachute Regiment who wished to retain the emblem; along with the tradition and pride that helps maintain the *esprit de Corps* of fighting units. Today, The Parachute Regiment still holds onto the tradition of Pegasus as the name for their regimental journal and their regimental mascot, a Shetland pony.

Out with the old and in with the new. In 1999 Pegasus ridden by Bellerophon was replaced with an eagle.

Pegasus Bridge was originally referred to, back in 1944, as Bénouville Bridge or the Caen Canal Bridge and was the first bridge captured on D-Day. This was by the men of B and D Coy of 2 Oxf Bucks, a detachment of Royal Engineers from 249 Fd Coy and the men of the Glider Pilot Regiment. Also situated on the south-west bank of the Caen Canal, just to the right of where you now stand is the:

2) *Café Gondrée.* Situated on the south-west bank of the Caen Canal near the new Pegasus Bridge, it was the first house to be liberated in France and above the entrance you will see a large white marble plaque:

Paratrooper with 'Pegasus', mascot of The Parachute Regiment.

3) *First Liberated House in France Plaque.* You will also notice that the sign reads that the house was liberated in the last hour of 5 June. This suggests that the local time was not adjusted for summer time and, as the Allied forces used double British Summer Time (BST) for their operations in Normandy; French time was thus one hour behind British time. Hence Allied records show the first landings taking place in the first hour of 6 June and French records show them taking place in the last hour of 5 June.

Below the white plaque there is a granite plaque:

4) 7 Para Plaque. This commemorates the relieving of Major John Howard's men by 7 Para and their CO Lieutenant Colonel Richard Geoffrey Pine-Coffin DSO, MC. The plaque records the time that 7 Para arrived as 0130hrs. 7 Para war diary records this time as 0140hrs. To the right, there is a granite plaque:

5) Aid Post Plaque. This was presented by the Glider Pilot Regimental Association in 2009. This memorial commemorates the use of the *Café Gondrée* as an aid post, from the night of 5/6 June, where shelter and medical treatment was given to casualties.

Georges Gondrée (left), Major John Howard (centre) and Lt David Wood (right) at Pegasus Bridge.

The café is now owned by Madame Arlette Gondrée-Pritchett who witnessed the battle as a four year old girl while living with her parents and her older sister, Georgette, in the café. Her parents Monsieur Georges and Madame Thérèse Gondrée worked actively for the French Resistance passing on vital information during 1944. It has also been said that Georges had received word on 5 June that his presence was required at the café for the next few days. Early next morning he realised why.

You will find the atmosphere of the café is particularly memorable as this is the only building or place around the new Pegasus Bridge that has been preserved in its original condition. Today the café is looked upon as a shrine by many of those who fought around here and over the years a wealth of memorabilia has been donated by 6th Airborne Division veterans. There is a good selection of souvenirs, books, maps, pictures and postcards for sale, the latter of which can be posted at the café, as well as the usual pleasant services offered by the traditional French café.

An additional bonus to your visit may be the chance to meet the charming Madame Arlette Gondrée-Pritchett herself, as she is often present at the café and is more than welcoming in answering any questions or posing for photographs outside for the thousands who visit her establishment throughout the year. One polite request made by Madame Gondrée-Pritchett is that no photographic or video recordings are taken inside the café. This continues a tradition started by her mother, with the sentiment that if anyone wishes to witness the unique collection of memorabilia inside the café, they can do so only by visiting and showing their respect in person.

It is worth noting that the café is generally closed out of season between the last week of November and the first week of March. Outside and back in the car park alongside the west side of the café is:

6) *No. 1 Special Service Brigade Memorial.* This unit was commanded by Brigadier Simon Fraser The Lord Lovat, and with him his Piper Bill Millin. The well known film *The Longest Day* shows Piper Millin playing his bagpipes while they crossed Pegasus Bridge for the first time. In reality this did not happen due to mortar and sniper fire in the area. However, despite still being under fire from the Germans, Piper Millin did play his pipes as they crossed Horsa Bridge. The plaque shows the time when the commandos joined forces with the airborne troops as

1202hrs 30 secs making the first link-up between the British airborne and seaborne troops on D-Day. However, 1 SS Bde HQ and 3 Cdo war diaries record the crossing of the bridges at 1230 hrs. Set back from the *Café Gondrée*, on your right is the:

7) *Café Gondrée annexe*. This is an extension of the café/museum dedicated to the 6th Airborne Division. This annexe includes more

Café Gondrée. Situated on the south-west bank of the Caen Canal.

memorabilia, as well as a conference and briefing room which may be used by visiting school parties, official organisations or military staff colleges. All information concerning the café and annexe can be obtained from Madame Arlette Gondrée-Pritchett Tel/Fax: 0033 (0)2.31.44.62.25. or Mobile Tel: 0033 (0)8.02.40.13.28. It was opened on the fifty-fifth anniversary of the landings in June, 1999. To the right of the entrance of the *Café Gondrée* car park, behind you, there is the:

8) *Pegasus Bridge Café Gondrée Signpost*. It was presented to Madame Arlette Gondrée-Pritchett, on 6 June 2002, by the Gloucester branch of the Parachute Regimental Association. The plaque also acknowledges the *Café Gondrée* as the first house in France to be liberated by the 6th Airborne Division, and its use as a Regimental Aid Post during the fighting for Bénouville. It was presented here to replace the original sign that was made in June 1944 by the Royal Engineers of the 6th Airborne Division and which is now in the Pegasus Memorial Museum.

Walk back towards Pegasus Bridge and, on the east side of the café, walk along the towpath, which follows the south-western bank of the Caen Canal, for approxiamately 600 yards (549m). On the left of the towpath beside the canal is:

9) *First Bailey Bridge Memorial Plaque*. Dedicated to 17, 71 and 263 Fd Coys RE. This stone marks the site of the first Bailey Pontoon Bridge that was built in France. This particular bridge was a 224ft (68.28m) Bailey Pontoon Class 40 Bridge. This

First Bailey Bridge Memorial Plaque.   **The same site in 1944.**

signified that it could withstand 40 tons (40.64 tonnes) in weight.

In total some five Bailey pontoon bridges would be built across the Caen Canal during the Normandy campaign. The first was called LONDON I and was completed on 8 June 1944. The original marker (whereabouts unknown) has been replaced with this brick and granite memorial. The other bridges over the Caen Canal were given the names of TOWER I and YORK I, between Ouistreham and Bénouville, and TAY I and CALIX, between LONDON I and Caen. On the opposite side of the towpath approximately 300 yards (274m) further south is:

10) *Bénouville Château.* Back in 1944, this eighteenth century château was being used as a maternity hospital and orphanage run by the fifty-four year old Madame Léa Vion. During June

Bénouville Château.

and July some eighteen children, reportedly all girls, were born in the château. Madame Vion had also helped the French Resistance and had offered sheltered protection to shot down Allied pilots and members of the French Resistance who were on the run from the Germans since the start of occupation.

On the 6 June she also protested vehemently with the Germans when they at one point during the battle attempted to use the château rooftop to site one of their machine-gun posts. After an artillery shell had hit the château the Germans decided to vacate the building for the rest of the battle.

This was also the building Corporal Wally Parr fired upon with the captured German anti-tank gun sited on the south-east corner of Pegasus Bridge. Not knowing that the château was being used to house women and children, Corporal Parr had suspected that the Germans were actually using the building as an OP. Years later Corporal Parr was amused to learn that someone else had received the blame for his bombardment. As he recalls:

> I was reading an article in Post, an American magazine. I was glancing through it, and there on one of the pages was a picture of Pegasus Bridge. I thought, that's the bridge I captured in Normandy so I started to read the article. The story included a passage that told how the cowardly Germans, in their retreat from the bridge, had deliberately shelled a château that was being used as a maternity hospital. This was the first and only time I had shelled pregnant women and newborn babies.
>
> CORPORAL WALLY PARR, 2 OXF BUCKS

Walk back towards the bridge and turn left, just past the *Café Gondrée*. Walking away from Pegasus Bridge along the path and at the end of the car park there is, on a white concrete plinth, a brass marker:

11) Airborne and Commando Memorial Marker.

Continue along the road up to the roundabout for approximately 220 yards (200m). This was originally a T junction in 1944 between Bénouville, le Port and the road leading to Bénouville (Pegasus) Bridge. This square is known as *Place de la liberation* and to your left is:

12) Bénouville Mairie (Town Hall). There is a marble plaque, on the wall to the left of the entrance door claiming it to be the first *Mairie* to be liberated in France in 1944. You will notice that the time inscribed on the plaque of 5 June 1944, 2345hrs refers to local time. However, 7 Para war diary shows that the battalion

did not drop onto DZ N until 0050hrs, and Lieutenant Colonel Pine-Coffin did not cross the canal bridge until 0140hrs. In front of the Mairie is the shattered remains of Bénouville's:

13) First World War Memorial. This was damaged during the fighting for Bénouville during the Normandy campaign. The memorial now has, on the front, memorial plaques for those killed in 1944.

Bénouville Mairie **and First World War Memorial damaged in 1944.**

Cross the road opposite the front of the Mairie and on the corner of the junction there is:

14) 7 Para Bn Memorial. This memorial is dedicated to all ranks of 7 Para who, as part of 5 Para Bde, were the first reinforcements for Major John Howard at Pegasus Bridge. 7 Para then went on to take and secure this area around Bénouville and le Port. The fighting for Bénouville was fierce and there was the ever present danger of sniper fire for anyone in the vicinity.

One officer who landed with 7 Para on D-Day was the now famous actor and movie star Richard Todd (right). He later went on to play the role of Major John Howard in the film *The Longest Day*. There was no depiction of Richard Todd's D-Day experience in the film.

> *By dawn we had a few mortar men and a few machine-gunners... their machine guns and mortars had gone. All they carried were pistols as side arms. The CO asked me to form a patrol out of these ex-mortar men and machine-gunners. The first thing he asked us to do was to go and look at C Coy which was further up towards the mouth of the canal towards Ouistreham. I went to the canal edge and a little further up I saw a helmet. You could just see it and the glint of a weapon – presumably a rifle – in a good covered firing position right up ahead of us. It was all open ground so I got the platoon to stop and take cover while I tried to go down the bank of the canal to see if I could come along behind it. I eventually did. It was one of our own chaps, dead. He was just lying there with his rifle and he had a little black hole just there in his forehead*

107

– dead as mutton with this rifle still in the aim.
LIEUTENANT RICHARD TODD, ADJUTANT, 7 PARA

The Commanding Officer of 7 Para, Lieutenant Colonel Richard G. Pine-Coffin, had left England with 640 men, but by first light on 6 June he only had 210 men. Sixty of these were accounted for as killed or wounded, while the rest were still missing after the drop. 7 Para were eventually relieved that evening by 2 Warwicks who had landed on SWORD Beach with the 3rd Infantry Division. 7 Para was then ordered back to the DZ and held in reserve. But the fighting was not yet over for 7 Para and by the end of the Normandy campaign their total casualties amounted to 452.

Continue along, past the 7 Para memorial and into le Port (which is still part of Bénouville), and stop after 400 yards (366m) at:

15) *Bénouville Church and Churchyard.* In the grounds of this church rest twenty-three men, the majority of whom were with the 6th Airborne Division and killed on 6 June. Amongst them is the padre for 7 Para, twenty-nine year old The Reverend George E.M. Parry. During the morning of D-Day the padre was helping tend the wounded in one of the RAPs that had been set up in a house in Bénouville. At one point some Germans, on patrol, entered the building in which The Reverend Parry was tending the wounded and a fight broke out. During the fighting a number of the wounded and medical staff were killed along with the padre.

Reverend George Parry.

Walk back towards Pegasus Bridge until you come to the café, restaurant and shop:

16) *Les 3 Planeurs.* Inside you will find photographs of the landings on the restaurant walls. Next door to the restaurant is a souvenir and bookshop. Outside, between the bookshop and Caen Canal, there is a:

17) *Centaur IV (A27L) tank.* This had been used by the Royal Marine Commando armoured support units that came ashore with 3 Inf Div on

SWORD Beach. This one was recovered from the beach at la Brêche d'Hermanville, in 1975 and was then restored by 60 Station Workshop REME, and placed here in 1977. The base upon which it stands was constructed by 34 Sqn RE.

Cross over the road and walk along the right-hand footpath over Pegasus Bridge. Stop on the east bank of the Caen Canal just before the end of the bridge. On your left, mounted on the railings is a brass:

18) *2 Oxf Bucks Commemoration Plaque.* This was erected by the Royal Green Jackets.

Continue walking and turn right onto the gravel covered east bank. This area is known as:

19) *Esplanade John Howard.* Named in honour of Major John Howard. To your right you will see the only remaining original piece of German military hardware in this area, it is an anti-tank gun:

20) *50mm (1.97in) Kwk anti-tank gun.* Mounted in its Tobruk pit this weapon, originally from a tank, was sited here as a static defence. However, it was moved a few yards to the east, away from its original position, when the Caen Canal was widened back in 1994. Between the row of flagpoles and the canal bank is a large stone:

21) *Comité du Débarquement Monument.* This is one of many monuments erected by the *Comité du Débarquement* (D-Day commemoration committee). These monuments are situated at various points along the Normandy landing beaches and drop zones. The committee, founded by Monsieur Raymond Triboulet, was set up on 22 May 1945. It is a non-profit association and is dedicated to preserving the memory of the Normandy invasion and tasked with managing the commemoration of the D-Day landings. This marker commemorates the glider landings here at Pegasus Bridge. Approximately 10 yards (9m) farther on is:

22) *'The Pegasus Trail' Orientation Table (1),* one of three such tables (see Ch. 7, A) that form part of *The Pegasus Trail*; an audio tour and booklet that was compiled by Lieutenant General Sir Michael Gray, KCB, OBE, FBIM, in 1989. He was also then the Chairman of the Airborne Assault Normandy Trust before becoming Joint President with Major Jack Watson MC.

This orientation table is one of three in the area of operations for the 6th Airborne Division.

Walk across to the other side of the flagpoles, and to the footpath that leads from the *esplanade* down to the glider memorials. At the top of the footpath to your left there is:

23) *OVERLORD l'Assault Marker*. This is one of many markers of a route called *OVERLORD l'Assault* (OVERLORD, The Assault). On each marker there is a brief explanation in both French and English of what happened in this particular area. This forms just one of eight such self-guided trails, provided by the *Comité Departemental Du Tourisme Du Calvados (CDT Calvados), CDT Manche* and *CDT Orne*, that covers the whole area of Normandy that is associated with the Normandy campaign. A free information booklet/map called *The D-Day Landings And The Battle For Normandy* can be picked up at most museums and tourist information outlets in Normandy. The first marker on this particular trail is situated at the Merville Battery (see

Battleground Europe book *Merville Battery & The Dives Bridges* see Ch. 5, D2) and finishes at the *Musée Mémorial de la bataille de Normandie* (Memorial for The Battle of Normandy Museum), in Bayeaux.

Now walk down the footpath that leads from the esplanade to the three glider landing memorials and stop at:

24) *Bronze Bust of Major John Howard*. This bust, the first of three sculptured by Vivian Mallock (see Ch. 7, B11 & Battleground Europe book *Merville Battery & The Dives Bridges* Ch. 5, D33) was presented to the mayor and people of Bénouville by the Airborne Assault Normandy Trust and the Oxfordshire and Buckinghamshire Light Infantry Association in 1994. To the left of the bust is:

25) *First Glider Landing Marker.* Approximately 80 yards (73m) from the bridge, this is one of three monuments and plaques that mark the exact position where the gliders came to rest in LZ X, aka EUSTON I. These replace the original lectern-like markers that were vandalised in the spring of 1998. The plaque on the marker gives the exact time of 0016hrs of when the first glider landed. One of the most compelling pieces of evidence for the accuracy of this time is Major John Howard's watch, which was broken on landing and had stopped at 0016hrs precisely. The first glider to land was glider No. 1 (667) which had the chalk mark of No. 91 written on the side of the fuselage. The chalked number was to help ground crews when hooking the gliders up to their tow. The glider's serial code was PF800. This had been towed over to Normandy by a Halifax bomber, serial LL355-G, from 298 Sqn 38 Group, piloted by Wing Commander D.H. Duder, DSO, DFC. There were also five more aircrew (for full roster of tug crew, glider crew and assault troops for *coup de main*, see Appendix F).

Also on the plaque are the names of the glider pilots, Staff Sergeants Wallwork and Ainsworth, and the names of Major John Howard and Lieutenant Den Brotheridge, the two officers of 2 Oxf Bucks who were in the glider on landing. Lieutenant Den Botheridge, after succumbing to the fatal wound he received while crossing over Pegasus Bridge (see Ch. 3 & 4), is recorded as the first British fatal casualty, as a result of enemy fire, on French ground during D-Day. He is now buried in Ranville churchyard (see Ch. 7, B4). In total there were twenty-eight troops (including five engineers) on board plus the two glider pilots.

Continue along the footpath until you come to the:

26) *Third Glider Landing Marker.* Approximately 130 yards (119m) from the bridge, it marks the spot where glider No. 3 (663), with the chalk mark No. 93, landed. The time was 0018hrs. The glider's serial code was LH469. This had been towed by a Halifax bomber, serial LL218-N, from 644 Sqn 38 Group, piloted by Warrant Officer J.A. Herman. There were also five more aircrew.

It was in the pond, directly behind the memorial, that Bren gunner Lance Corporal Fred Greenhalgh was thrown into on landing. Trapped by the wreckage of the glider, and most likely unconscious as a result of the impact, he is subsequently

Early photograph of the bridge and German gun position.

recorded as having drowned in the pond. He is thereby acknowledged as the first recorded British soldier to die on French soil on D-Day. He now rests in la Déliverande Commonwealth War Cemetery, Douvres (plot V, row C, grave 4). On the plaque the glider pilots, Staff Sergeants Barkway and Boyle, are mentioned along with the officers Lieutenant R.A. 'Sandy' Smith, 2 Oxf Bucks, and Captain John Vaughan (aka Jacob), RAMC, who were in the glider. The total complement on this glider was twenty-eight troops (including five engineers and one medical officer) plus two glider pilots. At the end of the path is the:

27) *Second Glider Landing Marker*. Approximately 165 yards (150m) from the bridge the time of landing for glider No. 2 (661), chalk mark No. 92 was 0017hrs. The glider's serial code was LW943. This had been towed by a Halifax bomber, serial LL335-K, from 298 Sqn 38 Group, piloted by Warrant Officer A.K. Berry. There were also six more aircrew.

On the plaque the glider pilots, Staff Sergeants Boland and Hobbs, along with the officers Lieutenant David J. Woods, 2 Oxf Bucks, and Captain H.R.K. 'Jock' Neilson, 249 Fd Coy RE, are commemorated. Again the full complement was twenty-eight troops (including five engineers and one medic) plus two glider pilots.

Return to the bridge and turn right, due east, onto the D514 and walk approximately 540 yards (494m) to the bridge, across the River Orne, which is now known as:

28) *Horsa Bridge*. Previously known as Ranville Bridge or the River Orne Bridge, this bridge is now named after the type of glider used during its capture, the Airspeed (AS) 51 Horsa Mk I. Like Pegasus Bridge this is not the original bridge. The original, a steel lattice swing bridge, was replaced in 1971.

Walk onto the bridge and look south; at low tide – approximately 100 yards (91m) away on the banks either side of the River Orne – you can see the remains of the original bridge supports:

29) *Bridge Support Remains*. As the River Orne is a tidal river these remains are only visible for up to twelve hours each day. At low tide you will be able to see wooden support poles. These once formed part of one of the many temporary bridges that were built over the River Orne during the Normandy campaign. This one was codenamed LONDON II. In total some seven Bailey bridges were built by British engineers between the mouth of the River Orne and Caen. These were given the names, from north to south, of: TOWER II, YORK II, EUSTON, LONDON II, TAY II, BUNCH and LAYR. Five additional bridges were also built in Caen itself after it was liberated. The names of these, again from north to south, were: REYNOLDS, CHURCHILL, MONTY, TICKELL and BARRET. For further information see the Bailey bridge exhibit in the Pegasus Memorial Museum (see Ch. 6, B20).

Walk across the roadway to the north-west corner of the bridge and to your left is:

30) *Horsa Bridge Memorial*. This memorial is dedicated to the glider pilots and troops of the two gliders who successfully landed near the bridge. Closest was glider No. 6 (664), chalk

mark No. 96, with the serial code PF791. It landed approximately 170 yards (155m) from the bridge only minutes after Major John Howard had landed at Pegasus Bridge. The area behind the memorial is LZ Y, aka EUSTON II, where the glider landed. The glider had been towed by a Halifax bomber, serial LL350-Z, from 644 Sqn 38 Group, piloted by Flying Officer W.W. Archibald. There were also five more aircrew. The other glider that managed to land nearby, approximately 850 yards (777m) from its objective and farther north, was glider No. 5 (660), chalk mark No. 95, with serial code

LJ326. This had been towed by a Halifax bomber, serial LL406-T, from 298 Sqn 38 Group, piloted by Warrant Officer G.P. Bain. There were also five more aircrew.

The memorial has inscribed the names of the glider pilots, Staff Sergeants Roy A. Howard and Frederick W. 'Freddie' Baacke and the names of Lieutenant Dennis Fox of 2 Oxf Bucks and Lieutenant Jack Bence of 249 Fd Coy RE, who were in glider No. 96. It acknowledges them as the officers leading the platoon and engineers to capture the bridge. The full complement of glider No. 96 was twenty-eight troops (including five engineers and one medic) plus two glider pilots.

Also mentioned on the memorial are the glider pilots, Staff Sergeants Stan Pearson and Len Guthrie and Lieutenant Henry J. 'Tod' Sweeney of 2 Oxf Bucks, all on board glider No. 5, chalk mark No. 95. The memorial acknowledges these troops as the second platoon to arrive and reinforce the troops at the bridge. The full complement for glider No. 95 was twenty-eight troops (including five engineers and one 7 Para liaison officer) plus two glider pilots.

There is no mention of the third glider, No. 4, chalk mark No. 94, as this was released by its tug too far to the east and landed just over 7 miles (11.27km) from its objective, next to a bridge over the River Dives in the area of the *Commune de Périers en Auge* (see Battleground Europe book *Merville Battery & The Dives Bridges* Ch. 8, A). This bridge is located some 2 miles (3.22km) to the east of the bridge over the River Divette, at Varaville. The Varaville Bridge being one of the six bridges the airborne engineers were tasked with demolishing.

Now walk back over Pegasus Bridge to your vehicle. Drive back over Pegasus Bridge and take the first left-hand turn onto *Avenue du Major Howard*. Park in the car park some 50 yards (46m) on your right, alternatively, if full, park in the car park some 100 yards (91m) further on to your left. The building here is the:

B. Memorial Pegasus Museum (*Musée Mémorial Pegasus*)
Through the main entrance, and into the entrance hall of the museum, you will see a number of exhibitions, photographs and paintings on the walls. To your left is a souvenir shop (that you will pass through as you exit the museum). In front of you is the desk at which you will need to pay an entrance fee to enter the museum to your right.

Musée Mémorial Pegasus.

The main exhibition hall of the museum contains a large collection of exhibits in the many display cases and open areas. There is a wealth of information and items of interest to be seen, including many photographs of the battlefields in 1944 and of the men who took part in those battles.

It is worth taking the time to go into the amphitheatre, situated in the centre of the exhibition hall, and watch the archive film, introduced by HRH The Prince of Wales. In the centre of the amphitheatre there is also a detailed model of this area of Normandy. A museum guide, at regular intervals, will explain the operations for the 6th Airborne Division using the model.

Amongst the many interesting objects in the exhibition hall is Major John Howard's steel airborne helmet, worn by him on D-Day. The bullet holes that can be clearly seen in the helmet were made when a German sniper fired at Major Howard while his unit was fighting in the village of Escoville on 7 June (see Battleground Europe book *Merville Battery & The Dives Bridges* Ch. 6, G). Fortunately, the bullet only grazed the top of his head. Also on display are Major Howard's D-Day red beret, his silk escape map, and his medals. These are: Distinguished Service

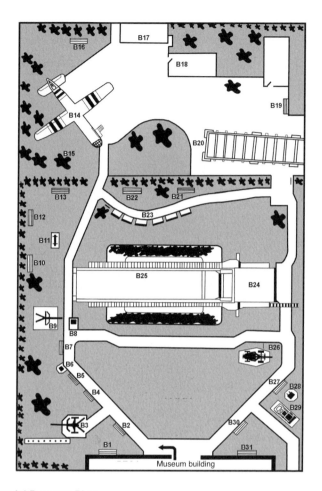

Memorial Pegasus Plan.

Order (DSO), 1939-45 Star, France and Germany Star, Defence Medal, War Medal 1939-45 and French Croix de Guerre. In the same display case there is also the hip flask which was being carried by Lieutenant Den Brotheridge when he made the assault across Pegasus Bridge.

In another display case there is the green beret of Brigadier The Lord Lovat's piper, Bill Millin, along with his famous bagpipes. Also in the exhibition hall are the original two copper plaques, one of the Pegasus emblem and the other with the simple inscription '6 JUNE 1944', from the memorial cross to the 6th Airborne Division that is located in Ranville Commonwealth War Cemetery (see Ch. 7, B2).

The rest of the exhibits in the exhibition hall cover nearly

116

every aspect of the airborne landings in Normandy, including: the preparations for the airborne landings, the capture of the bridges, the southern flank, the Merville Battery, resupply missions, the bridges over the River Dives and Divette, the eastern flank, advance towards the River Seine and other information on equipment, the gliders, parachutes, medical services and communication equipment.

After you have finished looking at the exhibits in the exhibition hall exit the building into the Memorial Pegasus Park. If you follow the footpath around to your left, this will lead you to many memorials and exhibits. First, on your left-hand side against the museum building is:

1) *12 Para Memorial Plaque*. This brass plaque, fixed to the top of the backrest of one of the bench seats, is dedicated to all ranks of 12 Para who gave their lives in Normandy. Next, along the footpath is a second bench seat. On the backrest is a brass plaque:

2) *6th Airborne Division Plaque*. Dedicated by the family of Placid R.P. Gonzales, 9 Para, to all ranks. Down a path, a short distance on your left is:

3) *5.5in (139.7mm) Medium Gun*. Used by most of the medium regiments of the Royal Artillery in the Second World War, the 5.5in (139.7mm) calibre gun could fire two to five rounds per minute. Rounds were made up of either 80lb (36kg) or 100lb (45kg) charges. Maximum ranges were 18,100 yards (16,551m), some 10.28 miles (16.55km) for a supercharged 80lb (36kg) shell, with a velocity of 1,950ft (594m) per second. For the 100lbs (45kg) shell, maximum range was 16,200 yards (14,813m), some 9.2 miles (14.8km), with a velocity of 1,675ft (511m) per second.

The gun's weight in action was 13,646lbs (6,190kg), some 6.09 tons (6.19 tonnes) and was usually towed by a Matador vehicle that would also carry the ammunition and essential mechanical spares and tools. Manned by a crew of ten men, a well trained crew could have this gun firing on target within three minutes of taking up firing positions. The accuracy, at 9 miles (14.48km), was within 6ft (1.83m). When used as an anti-tank weapon the crew would often fire a 100lb (45kg) shell, minus the fuse, but with the transit steel plug still in place. This would, with accurate fire, lift the tank turret from its mount. By the end of the campaign in north-west Europe, between 6 June 1944 and 8 May 1945, 21 Army Group fired 2,610,747 rounds with their 5.5in

Crew of a 5.5in. (139.7mm) in action.

(139.7mm) medium guns.

Back on the main path, to your left is a third bench seat. On the backrest is a brass:

4) *6th Airborne Division Memorial Plaque.* Dedicated to all ranks by St James' Place Foundation. On the fourth seat bench along the path the backrest has a brass:

5) *3 Para Bde Memorial Plaque.* Dedicated to all ranks who gave their lives from this unit. Next along the footpath is the:

6) *Brigadier James Hill DSO MC Bronze.* This bronze statue was first unveiled, on the eve of the sixtieth anniversary, on 5 June 2004 by HRH The Prince of Wales. At this time Brigadier James Hill was the highest ranking surviving D-Day officer of the 6th Airborne Division. The statue was originally positioned in the small park at le Mesnil crossroads (see Battleground Europe book *Merville Battery & The Dives Bridges* Ch. 6, E),

Brigadier James Hill DSO MC.

near the site where Brigadier Hill had his main headquarters on D-Day for 3 Para Bde (hence the description on the bronze plaque about 'this area'). After some unfortunate acts of vandalism, the statue was moved here to the memorial park for protection. Brigadier Hill passed away in March 2006 aged ninety-five years. Next along the footpath is:

7) 2 Oxf Bucks Memorial Plaque, situated on the backrest of a fifth bench seat, it is dedicated to all ranks of the 2 Oxf Bucks who fell whilst serving with the 6th Airborne Division. On the opposite side of the pathway, a few steps on is:

8) Memorial to Lieutenant H.D. Brotheridge, This bronze plaque is dedicated to the memory of Lieutenant Den Brotheridge and acknowledges him as the first British fatal casualty of enemy fire on D-Day (see Ch. 3 & 4, Ch. 6, Λ25 & Ch. 7, B4). Next, to your left, along the path is:

9) 25pdr Field Gun. The standard field gun used by the British and Commonwealth forces. This field gun weighed 3,968lbs (1,800kg), Some 1.77 tons (1.80 tonnes), in action and had the capability of firing a standard 25lb (11kg) high explosive (HE) shell 13,400 yards (12,253m), just over 7.6 miles (12km). It was also capable of firing smoke, incendiary, flare, star shell and armour-piercing shells. The latter had a velocity of up to 2,000ft (610m) per second and could penetrate 2.75in (69.85mm) of armour at 400 yards (366m). A six man crew was needed to operate the gun to its full firing capacity, although a four-man crew could readily keep the gun in operation. The gun was towed by a four wheel driven vehicle that would also carry

British Artillery 25pdr team engaged in a battery shoot at night.

ammunition and essential mechanical spares and tools.

Just behind the 25pdr, to the right on the grass, is a sixth seat bench, the backrest has a brass:

10) *RAF Memorial Plaque*, dedicated to all ranks of the RAF who gave their lives in the battle for Normandy. Back towards the path there is:

11) *Pegasus Bridge signpost*. This signpost was renovated by the Airborne Assault Normandy Trust in 1996 and was originally in position near the *Café Gondrée* next to the new Pegasus Bridge. After it was removed and placed here in the museum park a new sign, donated by the Gloucestershire branch of the Parachute Regiment Association, was erected in June 2003 next to the *Café Gondrée* (see Ch. 6, A1). The original sign, from 1944, can be seen in the museum exhibition hall.

Further along, on the grass, is a seventh seat bench, on the backrest there is:

12) *8th Parachute Battalion Memorial Plaque*, dedicated to all members of 8 Para who gave their lives while serving with 3 Para Bde. Further along on the grass area is an eighth seat bench, on the backrest is:

13) *Lieutenant General Sir Napier Crookenden KCB DSO OBE DL Memorial Plaque*. Dedicated to Lieutenant General Sir Napier Crookenden, by his friends and family, the plaque acknowledges him as commanding officer of 9 Para. On D-Day Major Napier Crookenden was the Brigade Major of 6 Airldg Bde and landed, in a Horsa glider, on DZ/LZ N on the evening resupply mission at 2100hrs on 6 June. To boost the morale of his men he brought along with him copies of that day's late edition of the *Evening Standard* which proclaimed the landing of airborne troops in France. Lieutenant Colonel Terence Otway, CO of 9 Para on D-Day, was wounded near the *Château St Côme* on 12 June 1944, by the 19 June, he had succumbed to those wounds and was evacuated. Major Napier Crookenden then assumed command of 9 Para. He continued to command 9 Para through the rest of the Normandy campaign, through the Ardennes German offensive in December 1944; and during the last Allied airborne assault in north-west Europe as part of the crossing of the River Rhine in March 1945, for which he was awarded the DSO. Lieutenant General Sir Napier Crookenden passed away in October 2002 aged eighty-seven years.
Go back to the path and continue along until you reach:

14) *Replica Airspeed (AS) 51 Horsa Mk I Glider*. No complete original Horsa glider survives today as all were either destroyed or used as salvage by the armed forces or by the local inhabitants for building material. *Mèmorial Pegasus* decided to commission the building of a full-size replica from the original plans used by the de Havilland aircraft company (now succeeded by BAE Systems). It has been given the serial code PF800, the same as the first glider to land at Pegasus Bridge. This glider was unveiled by HRH The Prince of Wales as part of the sixtieth anniversary celebrations on 6 June 2004. During the occasion the Prince also met and sat in the cockpit with Jim Wallwork, the pilot of glider No. 91 at Pegasus Bridge. Jim Wallwork was awarded the Distinguished Flying Medal (DFM) for his action on D-Day.

The Horsa glider was built by Airspeed Limited (founded in York, England in 1931). The company was subsequently acquired by de Havilland in 1940, but retained its own identity. Today its successor is BAE Systems plc. The Airspeed (AS) 51 Horsa Mk I had a length of 67ft (20m), a wingspan of 88ft (27m) and a height of 19ft 6in (6m). Its loaded weight was 15,500lbs (7,031kg), some 6.9 tons (7.03 tonnes). It could carry two glider pilots plus: twenty-eight assault troops, or combination of troops, a jeep and trailer, motorcycles, artillery or other supplies. It had a tow speed of approximately 150mph (241kmh) and gliding speed of approximately 100mph (161kmh).

To the front, right-hand side of the glider, at the base of the tree, there is a:

15) *Memorial Plaque to Tom Packwood*. This marble plaque is a memorial to Lance Corporal Tom Packwood, who was in No. 25 Platoon of D Coy 2 Oxf Bucks and landed at Pegasus Bridge in glider No. 91. Tom Packwood passed away in May 2006 aged 84 years. To the rear of the glider, near the hedgerow is a ninth seat bench, on the backrest is:

16) *Sergeant Ken J. Henesey Memorial Plaque*. Dedicated to Sergeant Ken Henesey who landed with Major General Richard N. 'Windy' Gale on to DZ/LZ N in the early hours of 6 June

Horsa Mk I Glider.

1944. Sergeant Henesey was part of the 6th Airborne Division Headquarters Defence Platoon (HQ Def Pl). They landed with Major General Gale in glider chalk marked No. 70, piloted by Major Billy Griffith, of English test cricket fame, and Staff Sergeant Major Mew. With Major General Gale were eleven other members of 6th Airborne Div HQ along with a Jeep and two motorcycles. Their tug pilot was Royal Australian Air Force (RAAF) pilot Wing Commander 'Frank' MacNamara VC, flying with 295 Sqn RAF. A few yards to the right of the seat is a display case containing an:

17) *Original Horsa Glider Fuselage Section*. This middle section of a Horsa fuselage was donated by The Museum of Army Flying at Middle Wallop, Hampshire, England (www.flying-museum.org.uk). Other cabins at the end of the park contain other exhibits and information about the gliders and Bailey bridges. To your right there are a number of exhibition huts. In the first, featuring details and information about the gliders and glider pilots, there is a brass:

18) *Memorial Plaque to Corporal Ted 'HAM & JAM' Tappenden*. Corporal Tappenden was the wireless operator who landed in glider No. 91 with Major John Howard. His job was to relay the code signal *Hello FOUR DOG, HAM and JAM, HAM and JAM* to signify that the bridges had been captured intact. This memorial is placed here, as it is near this spot that Corporal Tappenden sent that message in the early hours of 6 June. Beyond the other exhibition huts, is a tenth seat bench, on the backrest is:

19) *Royal Engineers Memorial Plaque*. Dedicated by the Airborne Engineers Association, in June 2007, to the memory of the Royal Engineers who gave their lives in Normandy. To the right of the seat bench is an:

20) *Original Section of Bailey Bridge*. This exhibit is part of one of the original bridges built in this area in 1944. In 1950 French civil engineers dismantled the bridge and moved it to form a crossing over the River Dives in the *Commune de Beaumais* between Falaise and St-Pierre-sur-Dives. In January 2001 it was

Corporal Ted Tappenden.

replaced by a new bridge and the *Commune de Beaumais* donated the Bailey bridge to the *Mémorial Pegasus* where it was rebuilt in 2002. After the Bailey bridge, follow the footpath around to the right. On the grass to your right is an eleventh seat bench, on the backrest is:

21) *13 (Lancashire) Para Memorial Plaque*. Dedicated to all ranks of 13 Para who gave their lives while serving with 5 Para Bde. Next along is a twelfth seat bench, on the backrest is:

22) *2 (Airldg) Oxf Bucks Memorial Plaque*. Dedicated to all ranks of 2 Oxf Bucks who served with the 6th Airborne Division. As the path snakes around there are six large white sandstone plinths at the end of which is a plaque telling you about:

23) *The Men in Gliders Memorial*. This memorial (below) was unveiled on 6 June 2009 by General Sir Richard Dannett, GCB CBE MC ADC Gen Chief of the General Staff. On each of the six stone memorials are the names of tug pilot, glider pilots and troops for each of the gliders that formed the *coup de main* assault teams for the attack on Pegasus and Horsa Bridges. The memorial was built by funds raised by the trustees of Project 65 and the members, friends and families of The Oxfordshire and Buckinghamshire Light Infantry (43rd and 52nd). It was done to help preserve the memory, some sixty-five years after the event, of 'the men in gliders'.

On the plinth dedicated to the men of glider No. 3, chalk marked No. 93, you will see the RAMC officer referred to is named Captain Jacobs. Jacobs was the birth name of Captain John Vaughan. During a meeting at Bénouville in 1992 with Mark Worthington, now the Memorial Pegasus curator, Captain Vaughan explained that he adopted his ancestral surname, during his service in the war, so that he would not be mistaken for a Jew if taken prisoner (for the complete list of names for the men in the gliders see Appendix F).

Walk back along the path, past the memorial stones on your right, and turn right at the end of the path and walk onto the:

24) *Original Pegasus Bridge*. As mentioned previously, this

bridge was moved just before the fiftieth anniversary, for several years it was left rusting in a nearby field until funds were raised to preserve it and move it here into the Memorial Pegasus Park. Shrapnel and bullet marks can still be seen today on the superstructure and along the sidewalls of the bridge. Halfway along the bridge there is a:

25) *Pegasus Bridge Memorial*. Dedicated in 2011, in honour of all those who sacrificed their lives for the liberation of Pegasus Bridge. Return to the path and turn right, on the grass area to your right is a:

26) *40mm (1.58in) Bofors Anti-Aircraft Gun*. Used by light anti-aircraft regiments of the Royal Artillery during the Second World War. The 40mm (1.58in) Bofors weight in action was 4,368lbs (1981kg) some 1.95 tons (1.98 tonnes) and was manned by a crew of eight men which could fire up to 120 rounds per minute. Firing a standard 2lbs (0.91kg) HE shell the maximum horizontal range was 10,800 yards (9,876m), just over 6.14 miles (9.87km). Maximum ceiling was 7,860 yards (7187m), just under 4.47 miles (7.18km). If fitted with a tracer-igniter the maximum ceiling, until the self destruction of the shell, was either: 3,400 yards (3109m), some 1.93 miles (3.11km); or 5,500 yards (5029m), some 3.13 miles (2.86km), dependent upon which type of tracer-igniter was fitted. However, at this height, only harassing fire was possible. Accurate aimed fire, restricted by the predictor and sighting system, was only possible up to a range of approximately 1,600 yards (1,463m), 0.91 miles (1.46km).

The gun was towed by a four wheel driven Bedford QLB (Quad, Long, Bofors), that had been specially adapted to carry a gun crew of eight plus the driver, ammunition cases and other essential equipment. A well-trained gun crew could set up the Bofors on its stabilisers and be ready for action within two minutes.

It was the men of F Troop (Tp), 318 Battery (Bty), 92 (Loyals)

Maurice Segal next to a Bofors 40mm (1.58) Anti-Aircraft Gun today and in uniform in 194

Light Anti-Aircraft Regiment Royal Artillery (92 LAA Regt RA) that were tasked with protecting Pegasus and Horsa Bridges from aerial attack after their capture by Major John Howard's men. Landing on SWORD Beach on 6 June along with the 3rd Infantry Division, F Tp had made its way to Bénouville by the evening of D-Day. At first light the following day they set up their six Bofors gun positions, covering the area from Bénouville across to the east side of Horsa Bridge. The troop was brought into action by 0730hrs when the *Luftwaffe* launched an aerial attack. For five days they fended off many more air attacks and were credited with seventeen of the German aircraft that were shot down in that area.

On 13 June 123 (London Rifles) LAA Regt RA landed on the Normandy beaches and moved up to take over the air defences around the two bridges. During their landings the unit suffered some casualties after being strafed by a German bomber. The unit were also under regular shell and mortar fire while stationed near the bridges, as veteran Gunner Maurice Segal recalls:

> *I was in the open when mortar shells were landing around me. I was approaching two graves. Two soldiers had been laid on the ground and covered with earth. I did not know them; they were not of my unit. Sticks had been crudely fashioned into crosses and stuck in the ground. A steel helmet with a hole through it was perched on top. I threw myself between the graves for protection.*
>
> *When the shelling subsided I put my hands on the grave and said thanks fellas and went my way. The next day a stretcher party arrived, uncovered the bodies, laid each on a stretcher, and then covered them with blankets leaving just their boot exposed. I can still see in my mind's eye the boots receding into the distance and I feel guilty over my flippant remark.*
>
> GUNNER MAURICE SEGAL,
> B TP 405 BTY 123 LAA REGT RA

Further along the path on the left-hand side is a thirteenth seat bench, on the backrest is:

27) *1 RUR Memorial Plaque*, dedicated to all ranks of 1 RUR who fell while serving in the 6th Airborne Division. Next along the path, to your left is:

28) Quadruple 12.7mm (0.50in) Anti-Aircraft Gun Mounting. This would have originally been mounted on the rear of a half-track. Next along the path, also on the left is:

29) M3 A1 Half-Track. The A1 suffix indicates that the vehicle can be fitted with a ring-mounted 12.7mm (0.50in) calibre machine gun just above the cab. All vehicles had four-speed gearboxes and were fitted with two-speed transfer boxes and drive to both the tracks and front axle. Fuel consumption was an average of 2.73 miles per gallon (1km per litre). There were many variants widely used by the Allied forces. In total some 41,170 were built and put into service during the Second World War.

Continue along the path until you come to the fourteenth seat bench, on the backrest is:

30) RAMC Memorial Plaque, dedicated to all ranks of the RAMC who served with the 6th Airborne Division. Next, along the path to your left on the grass up against the museum building is a fifteenth seat bench. On the backrest is:

31) 1 Cdn Para Memorial Plaque. Dedicated to all ranks who served with 1 Cdn Para Bn of 3 Para Bde.

From here, at the end of the path, you can make your way back into the museum. To your right, after you enter the exhibition hall is the exit that will take you into the book and gift shop.

When you have finished your tour around the museum, return to your vehicle. The tour can be continued by following the directions in the next chapter.

CHAPTER SEVEN

Memorial Tour of Battlefield No. 2

Ranville

Distance between stops by vehicle: 1.6 miles (2.57km)
Total walking distance at stops: Approx 2 miles (3.22km)
Recommended time allowed for tour: 1 to 2 hours

Drive back down *Avenue du Major Howard* and take a left turn onto the D514 road heading east across Horsa Bridge. Take the third exit (D514), at the roundabout. Drive to the top of the hill and take the first sharp right signposted Ranville. Park on the grass verge just after the semi-circular orientation table on your right. The area to your left is:

A. DZ/LZ N (North) & 'The Pegasus Trail' Orientation Table (2)
This is the area where 5 Para Bde landed in the early hours of 6 June, followed by part of 6 Airldg Bde landing on the evening resupply mission on the evening of D-Day. The Pegasus Trail orientation table, the second of three, will help you identify local landmarks. The third orientation table is situated just under 1.5 miles (2.41km) away, to the SE, across the open fields on the far side of DZ/LZ N near Hérouvillette (see Battleground Europe

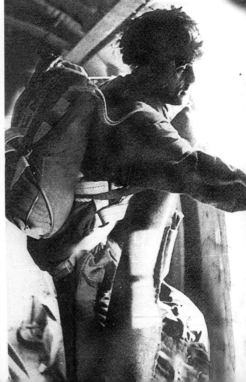

Brigadier Nigel Poett.

book *Merville Battery & The Dives Bridges* Ch. 6, F1).

One of the first men to land here was the commander of 5 Para Bde, Brigadier Nigel Poett. He landed with the pathfinders of 22 (Ind) Para Coy whose job it was to guide in the following aircraft by marking the DZ/LZ with radar beacons and coloured lights. Some thirty to forty minutes later 7, 12 and 13 Para were dropped here but were unfortunately scattered both on and around the DZ/LZ.

My chute developed normally, and as my body swung into the vertical I looked around... To my front, but some distance away numbers of red and orange balls were shooting up into the sky. This display I reasoned was the ack-ack defence of Caen. I stared at them far too long, because when I finally looked down, much to my horror it seemed I was destined to land in one of the orchards bordering the eastern side of the DZ... I prepared myself for a tree landing. I had never made such a landing, but I remembered what to do; head down on the chest, arms crossed in front of it, and knees raised to protect my marriage prospects. Down I came, crashing through branches and foliage, without so much as a scratch or bruise, but when I stopped falling and opened my eyes, I was completely surrounded by greenery. I felt around for a branch to get my feet on, but found none, So I turned the quick release on the parachute harness, gave it a bang, the straps flew apart, and my Sten which was broken into three parts, and threaded under them, fell to the ground. I slid out of the harness, keeping a tight grip on it, lowered myself to the end of the leg straps, and I hadn't reached the ground and was still enclosed in the foliage. I let go of the webbing harness, and dropped all of twelve inches [305mm] to the soil of Normandy.
LIEUTENANT ELLIS 'DIXIE' DEAN, 13 PARA

Only sixty per cent of 13 Para had made the RV before B and C Coys set off towards their objective which was to secure and hold the village of Ranville. They would also, along with 12 Para, deny the enemy the southern approaches to the river and canal bridges. Meanwhile A Coy, of 13 Para, was assigned the task of helping the sappers of 591 Para Sqn RE, in the clearance of the anti-glider poles that covered the DZ/LZ. Initially two

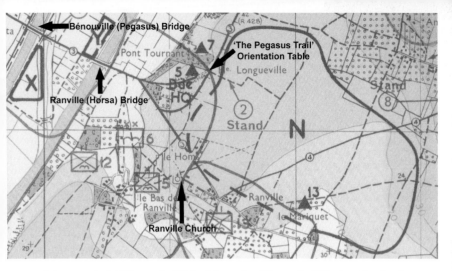

Bénouville (Pegasus) Bridge

Pont Tournant

'The Pegasus Trail' Orientation Table

Longueville

Ranville (Horsa) Bridge

le Hom

le Bas de Ranville

Ranville

le Mariquet

Ranville Church

strips, each 1,000 yards (914m) long by 60 yards (55m) wide, had to be cleared and ready for the glider landings that were to take place before dawn just over two hours later. These strips, when completed, would then be illuminated with lights by the pathfinders. As you stand with the orientation table in front of you, you are looking west across the breadth of DZ/LZ N. The two illuminated landing strips ran from left to right across the western side of this area.

Major J. Cramphorn's company from 13 Para was detailed as an infantry working party made up of four officers, twelve NCOs and 120 ORs. Before their arrival two Royal Engineer reconnaissance parties were to have taped out the landing strips. However, only one arrived on the DZ in time, but nevertheless managed to mark out both areas with frugal use of these limited tapes.

With cover provided by a protection party from 13 Para, the men began to clear the two strips. This involved the demolition and removal of a complete row of

Major J. Cramphorn.

anti-glider poles in each strip. Once cleared, each would provide enough room for thirty-five Horsa gliders to land.

There remained the problem of dropping the poles and then removing them. Permission was obtained to fell some 100 trees in the New Forest, something unheard of in peacetime, and these were then transported to Bulford Fields on Salisbury Plain where

129

they were erected according to the pattern in the air photographs. Following trials of various possible methods a standard drill was evolved as follows:

(a) The ground around the base of each pole was excavated to a depth of 6in [152.4mm] and about 12ins [304.8mm] out from the pole.

(b) A 5lb [2.27kg] sausage of plastic explosive was attached round the base of the pole to be fired by safety fuse and igniter. These sausages were made up in bicycle inner tubes and carried down by the parachute engineers as bandoliers.

Horsa gliders scattered among the dreaded anti-glider landing poles.

(c) Each pole was then removed by human porterage provided by an infantry working party and the shallow crater filled in and stamped down. Demolished poles were carried away to the side of the strip and laid at the base of a standing boundary pole and at 45 degrees to the axis of the strip to allow gliders to turn off. Six infantry teams of twelve men were required for each strip and they were headed by a RE NCO to ensure a safe separation from the demolition parties.

LIEUTENANT FRANK LOWMAN, CRE 6TH AIRBORNE DIVISION

'The Pegasus Trail' Orientation Table to the left of Drop Zone N alongside the D 514.

DZ/LZ N   Site of 'The Pagasus Trail'   Ranville Church   Site of Ranville
Orientation Table (2)   CWGC Cemetery

Z

Bénouville
(PEGASUS)
Bridge

Glider No. 92

Glider No. 93

Glider No. 91

Café Gondrée

Glider No. 96

Ranville
(HORSA)
Bridge

Bailey
Bridge
LONDON II

In training each strip took one and a half hours to clear. This target time was also achieved on D-Day, despite being under fire from German patrols. This was partially due to the fact that many of the poles were of a smaller diameter than expected and the strips were ready for the first wave of gliders with time to spare. However, the lighting of the strips proved inadequate since some of the specialised equipment had been destroyed or lost in the drop and subsequently the gliders came in from all directions for their landing. Fortunately, though, casualties and accidents were few.

> *The whistling sound and roar of the engines suddenly died down; no longer were we bumping about, but gliding along on a gloriously steady course... Round we turned, circling lower and lower; soon the pilot turned round to tell us to link up as we were just about to land. We all linked up by putting our arms round the man next to us. We were also strapped in. In case of a crash this procedure would help us take the shock. I shall never forget the sound as we rushed down in our final steep dive, then we suddenly flattened out, and soon with a bump, bump, bump, we landed on an extremely rough stubble field. Over the field we sped and then with a bang we hit a low embankment. The forward undercarriage wheel stove up through the floor, the glider spun round on its nose in a small circle and, as one wing hit one of those infernal stakes, we drew up to a standstill.*
>
> MAJOR GENERAL RICHARD GALE, GOC 6TH AIRBORNE DIVISION

As soon as all the gliders had landed and unloaded on the LZ the Royal Engineers and paratroopers began to work on two more landing strips, this time on the eastern side of the LZ. These were for the evening landings of 6 Airldg Bde. Since this landing included a greater number of Hamilcar gliders these strips had to be 90 yards (82m) in width, which meant an extra row of poles had to be removed. This task was completed by 0500hrs. But not everyone who was tasked with clearing the LZ had landed on or made it to the DZ.

> *I did not recognize the piece of ground I landed on, so I shinned up a signpost, thoughtfully left by the French, and struck a match to see where I was. It was almost two miles [3.22km] from where I was supposed to be. All around was the thudding of army boots as more men came down, and as there was not much 'asparagus' in my neighbourhood I used the*

Horsa glider, chalk mark No. 70, in which Major General Richard Gale landed. Below right his commemorative bronze bust.

explosive strapped around my waist to blow up a telegraph pole across the road to deter enemy reinforcements, which must have been tiresome to our troops who had to remove it later... After comforting a parachutist who was moaning in a ditch from a broken leg and whom I had no means of helping, I saw Lieutenant Colonel Luard who was rallying his men with a hunting horn... [later] an engineer major offered me a lift in his jeep which was scheduled to go to Troarn and blow up bridges, but thankfully I declined as it was the wrong direction. On the way to Ranville, where the château was to be Div HQ, I came across the divisional commander, General Gale, who had just arrived in his glider. It was near a crossroads and the general ordered a sergeant to clear some men from the crossroads, always a dangerous spot from enemy artillery. The man foolishly replied that they were not his men. General Gale exploded: 'What! Shamus, [Hickie, AA & QMG] here's a man arguing with Richard Gale!' Needless to say a frightened sergeant rapidly did as he was told.

Major General Richard Gale.

<small>MAJOR ANTHONY WINDRUM, ADJUTANT 6TH AIRBORNE DIVISION SIGNALS</small>

In the meantime 12 Para, with barely fifty per cent of its men, had set off on its task which was to take and hold the area south of Ranville around *le Bas de Ranville* and thereby protecting the southern approaches to the DZ, Ranville and the bridges over

German MG team covering a road junction as they seek to contain the British paratroopers.

the river and canal. 12 Para were in their positions ready to ward off any German attack by 0400hrs with only the hospitality of the local Normandy people holding them up.

We reached our objective, le Bas de Ranville village, where a French lady came from her farmhouse, which was on the land where we were digging in. Not being able to understand the French language very well, I could only guess that she was

*asking who we were and what we were doing. In the little French
I knew, I told her we were British and that this was the invasion.
She went back into her farmhouse and minutes later came out
with a jug of milk and some bread. I had a block of chocolate in
my camouflaged Denison smock which I gave to her.'*

CORPORAL R. DIXON, 12 PARA

But it was not long before the battle started and 12 Para were
soon engaged with advancing German patrols. In one of these
was Captain John Sim, with twelve of his men, entrenched in a
hedgerow, assisting a FOB pick out suitable targets for their
offshore cruiser to fire at. A German patrol spotted them and,
with two SP guns in support, they overpowered the small group
of paratroopers in a fierce firefight. Captain Sim was forced to
retreat, but only three of his men were able to accompany him.
Later the position was retaken with reinforcements and the
German SP guns destroyed by artillery.

As the wounded were collected by stretcher bearers Captain
Sim, who was later awarded the Military Cross for his action

Bren gun team guarding the landing zone.

that day, collected the dead and took them to Ranville churchyard. Today eight of them are still buried in the grass bank surrounding the churchyard. Later it was discovered that another man, who was in charge of a Bren gun position, had also escaped from the carnage. However, he was later taken prisoner.

The Germans now rushed a tank along the lane to our right with infantry on the top of it. There seemed to be a lull in the fighting and I began to think of our situation, which was that there were two of us left alive in the hedgerow. I decided to order Private Gradwell with his Bren to the rear, then I would follow him. He refused to retreat, saying, 'I'm not bloody going anywhere' and took up a firing position behind a fallen tree

British prisoners: Lance Corporal Frank Gleeson, front left, 12 Para, after he had been taken prisoner. Also taken as prisoners were medics from the parachute field ambulance who had remained with the wounded.

trunk. After several more orders to move, which he refused, I stood up and kicked him in the ribs. He then picked up the Bren and ran along the ditch that Captain Sim had used. I then decided to move back myself... I started to crawl back through the field of wheat which was nearly 3ft [0.9m] high. But under a clear blue sky I began to lose direction. So I decided to crawl back towards the roadside ditch. I moved the wheat stalks aside and dropped into the ditch, about a yard in front of a German machine-gunner and three others who were using the ditch to advance towards our main company position.

LANCE CORPORAL FRANK GLEESON, 12 PARA

B. Ranville

Return to your car and follow the road down into Ranville. As you pass the village sign you will see beneath it another sign acknowledging that the district was liberated by the 6th Airborne Division on the night of 5/6 June, 1944. In the distance you can see Ranville Church.

Continue down into the village and go straight across at the crossroads. Take the next left along the *Chemin de Longueville* and onto the *Rue des Airbornes*. This will take you to the front of Ranville Church. Follow the road round to the left, take the first road off the mini-roundabout and on the left-hand side are some parking spaces. To your right is the entrance to:

1) *Ranville Commonwealth War Cemetery*. As you walk through the gateway and under the stone entrance arch you will see, to your left, a small brass door above a stone seat. In here is kept the cemetery register, cemetery map and visitor's book. The cemetery register lists in alphabetical order all those known to be buried in this cemetery with Commonwealth nationals listed first, followed by foreign nationals.

In total 2,236 commonwealth nationals are buried in this cemetery including: 2,058 identified and ninety-seven unidentified from the United Kingdom; of whom ninety known and nine unknown are from the Royal Navy, 1,945 known and eighty-four unknown from the Army, twenty-three known from the Royal Air Force, two unknown from the Merchant Navy and two of unknown service. There are also seventy-six Canadians; of which sixty-seven known are from the Canadian Army and nine known are from the Royal Canadian Air Force; two known Australians from the Royal Australian Air Force; and three known from the Royal New Zealand Air Force.

In addition there are also 328 foreign nationals including; one known from the Belgian Army; five known from the French Army; one known from the Polish Army; and 213 known and 106 unknown from the German Army and two known from the German Air Force.

In total some 2,564 burials which are all maintained by the Commonwealth War Graves Commission (CWGC). If looking

for a particular individual, the location of their grave is given at the end of their entry in the register. You can then use the map at the front of the register to find each location within the cemetery grounds. All visitors are welcome to put their own personal entry in

Ranville War Cemetery in 1944.

Memorial Cross to the 6th Airborne in 1944. Inset: the author's daughter Michaela stands in for Sapper Hanslip in this comparison.

the visitors' book after their visit.

In the centre of the cemetery, you will see the large Cross of Sacrifice, there is one of these in each of the eighteen Commonwealth War Cemeteries that were constructed for casualties from the Normandy campaign. Just to the left of the Cross of Sacrifice, is:

2) *Memorial Cross to the 6th Airborne Division.* As with the signpost at Pegasus Bridge, it was Lieutenant Colonel Frank Lowman who had approached Major General Gale and also the Senior Chaplain, George Hales, with the design and idea for the cross. Permission was granted and the cross was made by Sapper Hanslip of 286 Fd Pk Coy RE. Using cement, he sprinkled the mould with coal dust to simulate marble. The two

RANVILLE
CWGC CEMETERY

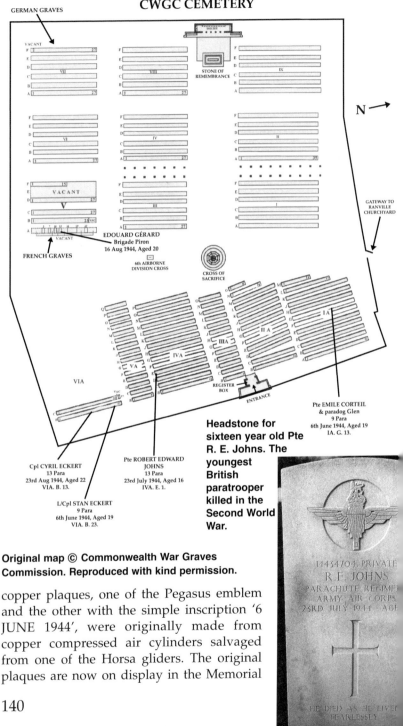

GERMAN GRAVES

VACANT

STONE OF
REMEMBRANCE

N →

GATEWAY TO
RANVILLE
CHURCHYARD

VACANT

V

VACANT

EDOUARD GÉRARD
Brigade Piron
16 Aug 1944, Aged 20

FRENCH GRAVES

6th AIRBORNE
DIVISION CROSS

CROSS OF
SACRIFICE

VIA

REGISTER
BOX

ENTRANCE

Pte EMILE CORTEIL
& paradog Glen
9 Para
6th June 1944, Aged 19
IA. G. 13.

Headstone for sixteen year old Pte R. E. Johns. The youngest British paratrooper killed in the Second World War.

Cpl CYRIL ECKERT
13 Para
23rd Aug 1944, Aged 22
VIA. B. 13.

Pte ROBERT EDWARD
JOHNS
13 Para
23rd July 1944, Aged 16
IVA. E. 1.

L/Cpl STAN ECKERT
9 Para
6th June 1944, Aged 19
VIA. B. 23.

copper plaques, one of the Pegasus emblem and the other with the simple inscription '6 JUNE 1944', were originally made from copper compressed air cylinders salvaged from one of the Horsa gliders. The original plaques are now on display in the Memorial

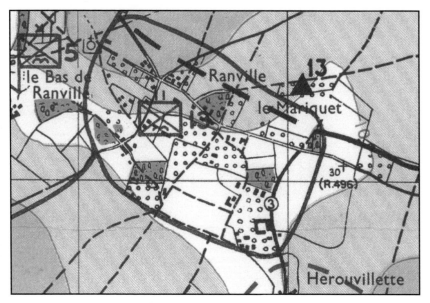

Pegasus Museum (see Ch. 6, B). The cross is surrounded by glider lashing chains that are held in place by brake fluid casings. As the, then temporary, divisional burial ground began to fill up the cross was erected and the ground consecrated by the Senior Chaplain on 24 June, 1944. The cross has since been moved from its original position to where it now stands today. After the war it was decided that the cemetery would become a permanent resting place for those buried here. Today, because of the number of airborne casualties interred, Ranville Commonwealth War Cemetery is still referred to as the 6th Airborne Division, or Airborne, Cemetery.

Also in the cemetery, although periodically repositioned, are two wooden benches, one donated by the Thanet branch of the PRA and the other with a memorial plaque dedicated to 8 Para.

As you walk around the cemetery you will see that the headstones for those who are identified from the Commonwealth forces can provide a great deal of information about the individual. There will be their name, rank service number and their regimental service or unit badge carved into the headstone. For those of the Jewish faith there will also be a Star of David and for those of the Christian faith a Latin cross. Beneath, at the base of the headstone there will usually be an inscription, penned or chosen, by the next of kin. But perhaps the most striking information given is the ages of the young men who now rest in this cemetery.

Over to the left-hand side of the cemetery the French graves are marked with a cross and a plaque; the Belgian headstone is a similar shape to the Commonwealth headstone; and the Polish headstone is also similar but with a more pointed peak. In the far left-hand corner of the cemetery are located the German graves, again similar to the Commonwealth headstones but with a sharp, rather than rounded, peak at the top of the headstone.

Brothers Corporal Cyril and Lance Corporal Stan Eckert.

It may seem insensitive to select people who now rest in this cemetery for particular mention, as it is important to remember that all these men were individuals; each with a family and story of their own. Nevertheless it seems fitting to at least give the reader and visitor alike a brief insight into the type of personalities that now rest here and detail, without prejudice, a few of the many.

Among the fallen is Private Robert Edward Johns (plot IVA, row E, grave 1) who represents the youngest British paratrooper killed in the Second World War, if not indeed the youngest British soldier. Serving with 13 Para his unit liberated and secured the village of Ranville on D-Day. Private Johns was killed six weeks later on 23 July 1944. Only after his death was it discovered that he had given a false age so

Private George White (left) and Lance Corporal Stan Eckert.

that he could enlist for the armed forces. He joined up aged only fourteen years old and when killed he was found to be only sixteen years old.

Also buried here are two brothers; twenty year old Corporal Cyril Albert James Eckert (VIA, B, 13) of C Coy 13 Para, and nineteen year

old Lance Corporal Stanley George Thomas Eckert (VIA, B, 23) of C Coy 9 Para.

Corporal Cyril Eckert was seriously wounded during an attack at Pont l'Evéque in August. Using an old door as a makeshift stretcher, he was then carried off the battlefield by his comrades. Despite being under fire, they managed to get him across the River Touques and to relative safety. He was then taken by ambulance to receive urgent medical attention. However, he succumbed to his wounds and died on 23 August. Initially he was buried in a small temporary burial ground in the village of St Hymer, to the south of Pont l'Evéque, later he was reinterred at Ranville.

There are many other heroic and tragic stories that could be told about those who now rest in this cemetery. One of the most heart-rending is that regarding a letter written by Corporal Cyril Eckert's younger brother, nineteen year old Lance Corporal Stan Eckert, to his mother on 6 June. A copy of the letter, and a photograph of the brothers can now be seen in the Merville Battery Museum (see Battleground Europe book *Merville Battery & The Dives Bridges* Ch. 5, D). The letter though is now faded with age and barely legible. What follows is a transcript:

Somewhere in France.

Dear Mum,

I am writing this letter at the bottom of a ditch very near the front line and I hope to get it posted pretty soon as my pal and I have a good idea that tomorrow we will be prisoners of war. I am writing this short note here so as if it is ever found by anyone they can forward it for me.

Do you know mum dear, I have never realised how much you meant to me, until now? If I can get home again, you will see a very different Stan, just wait and see. The same goes for dad, too, and the rest of the Eckerts. There is one thing that worries me, and that is what happened to Cyril. I hope and pray that he is safe and well.

Well, mum, just sit and wait for the end of the war when I will be 'home' once again, for good. Don't worry at all, will you.

With love to everyone at home, especially you.

Your ever loving son.

Stan   XXXXX

Lance Corporal Stan Eckert would never see his mother again. Stan died on D-Day. His body was found by a Royal Marine

Pte Emile Corteil and his paradog 'Glen'.

Headstone for Pte E. S. Corteil and his paradog 'Glen' buried with him.

commando, who discovered the letter and it was eventually passed on to the family. Initially the family received a telegram informing them that their son Stan was missing in action. Within seven weeks the family received yet more tragic news when a second telegram arrived informing them that Cyril had been killed in action.

Stan's body though was not recovered until much later, by which time his brother Cyril had already been laid to rest in Ranville. For this reason the two brothers, although in the same row, are not buried beside each other. Also killed on 6 June, and buried nearby, is Stan's closest friend in 9 Para, twenty-one year old Private George Vincent White (VA, E, 2).

In Ranville cemetery rests a body that is unique to any of the CWGC's 2,500 worldwide cemeteries; this is a body of a dog. Called 'Glen' he landed with his keeper, nineteen year old Private Emile 'Jack' S. Corteil (IA, G, 13). Glen, ironically a German Shepherd, was both the battalion mascot and a well trained sniffer dog used to smell out explosives, detect people and carry messages. He was also a trained paradog, and was fitted with his own parachute for his landing in Normandy in the early hours of 6 June. Sadly both Private Corteil and his companion 'Glen' were killed on D-Day (see Battleground Europe book *Merville Battery & The Dives*

144

Bridges Ch. 4) in what is known in military parlance as a 'blue on blue' incident. Today it is more commonly known as friendly fire.

It was Private Corteil's CO, Major Allen Parry, that decided that since the two were so devoted to each other they should be buried together. Private Corteil's mother wrote the epitaph for the base of the headstone.

Ranville is also the final resting place for the first and youngest Belgian soldier to be killed in Normandy, twenty year old Edouard Gérard (V, A, 12) who served with *Brigade Piron*. He was killed on 16 August 1944 (see Ch. 7 B8, B18 and Battleground Europe book *Merville Battery & The Dives Bridges* Ch. 5, A2, A3, B5 & D21).

For one paratrooper who survived the war, Ranville cemetery is a particularly memorable place. Not just for the reason that it is the place where many of his comrades now rest.

It was right here I landed… [between the memorial cross and the southern perimeter of the cemetery] *We were in a stick of about twenty, inside, the hole was in the middle* [of the aircraft] *so you're either side. Then one goes, another goes, alternatively jumping down and you're shuffling tight up behind one another to stay as close as possible, so you could very quickly get out. And the idea was you wouldn't land too far apart from one another. In actual fact we were pretty good, because when we dropped near Ranville I dropped and within a few moments I'd caught up with at least three and the fourth one had hit the churchyard wall and broke his arm. It was Thompson. What we did was take his morphine and we injected him with his own morphine. We didn't know to what extent his injuries were. And I always worried what had happened to him, taken prisoner or*

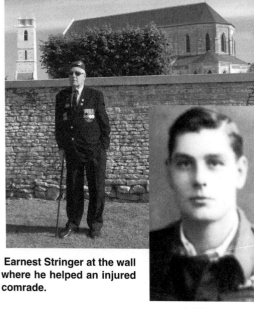

Earnest Stringer at the wall where he helped an injured comrade.

145

shot or what had happened to him 'cos obviously he was in a bad way and we had to leave him in the pitch dark...

We eventually picked up some others around the church and there was a good five of us initially, and we made our way into Ranville. We came round by the church up a lane and we met some more, an NCO and somebody, and made our way, single file down towards the bridges. It was still dark and what I really remember is the noise, banging and terrific noise going on. Obviously the Germans were coming back at the bridges already. And we were going towards it. We ran across the bridges and then separated along the banks.

[After the war] I was up at a reunion and talking to this chap [7 Para veteran] Ron Perry and I said to him 'this chap I've always been worrying about, and has been on my mind for many, many years, Thompson' and he said 'oh, he's still alive'... he'd smashed many bones in his arm and had to have lots of operations... He told me he became his best man at his wedding and he'd kept in touch with him... 'Cor, gee whizz', I said, 'I didn't know what had happened to the poor bugger'.

PRIVATE ERNEST 'ERNIE' STRINGER, HQ COY, 7 PARA

For nineteen year old Private Stringer, the intense fighting in and around Bénouville lasted only for a day or so until he was wounded; a bullet having gone through the side of his left foot. Private Ron Perry, after the war, told Private Stringer that he had been treated for his wounds in the cellar of the *Café Gondrée*. After his treatment at the RAP, he was evacuated to the beaches and then back to the UK.

146

Along the churchyard wall where Thompson had his unfortunate landing, there is a gate that leads through into:

3) *Ranville Churchyard.*

Through the gate, and to the right, a cinder path leads towards the front entrance of the churchyard. After passing the entrance gates on your right you will see, in front of the churchyard's low boundary wall a further forty-eight white CWGC headstones.

Among those buried here is one person with a headstone unique to any other CWGC headstone in Normandy in that it bares the inscription 5 June 1944. This headstone is for twenty-three year old Bombardier Henry 'Nobby' Hall (grave 19) of 53 Airldg Lt Regt RA. It is not known for certain if or how he was actually killed on 5 June 1944. No surviving veterans have been found who can recall how he met his fate. One comrade from 212 Bty of 53 Airldg Lt Regt RA, however, does recall the time Bombardier Hall received some unexpected news when back in the UK.

> *Nobby was not with us long before he received a posting out of the regiment, this was against his wishes and he was informed that the only way he could stay was to volunteer to become a parachutist... Nobby completed his course and took part in exercises. In one particular exercise on a night jump he landed in a tree, fortunately suffering only superficial injuries. He went off with the rest of the lads to prepare for the invasion.*
>
> GUNNER JAMES B SAUNDERS, TECHNICAL ASSISTANT
> 212 BTY 53 (WY) AIRLDG LT REGT RA

Bombardier Hall went on to train as a Parachutist FOO signaller and would form part of the 53 Airldg Lt Regt Forward Observation Section (FOS) and Airborne Support Net (ASN). This unit would relay targets for the regiment's three batteries of 3.7 inch (75mm) pack howitzers as the battery took up its position to the east of Pegasus Bridge. They would also later provide information for other artillery units as they came into the line. The FOS was split into twelve parties consisting of three men, comprising of one officer and two signallers; parties were then attached to 6th Airborne Division's HQ, brigades and their respective battalions. A party was also attached to 1 SS Bde and later they would also provide support for the 51st Highland Division.

One of Bombardier Hall's closest friends, Gunner David 'Dai' King, also a FOO signaller in 53 Airlanding Lt Regt RA, recalls the final time they were together.

> *The last time I saw Nobby was the end of May 1944. We were then sent to the respective transit camps ready for D-Day. We didn't know which para battalion we would be dropping in with, as you can imagine security was a priority.*
>
> GUNNER DAVID 'DAI' KING, SIGNALLER
> 53 AIRLDG LT REGT RA

Gunner David King, attached to 3 Para Bde HQ, was to land in the same drop zone as 8 Para. But no official records have yet been found regarding which unit Bombardier Hall was attached to, or indeed when and where he landed. Suggestions have been made that Bombardier Hall was reassigned to SAS or even SOE units that were dropped before the 6 June. However, in consideration of the lack of any evidence to support this, no conclusive answer can yet be given as to whether the mysterious and unique date on his headstone is actually correct or to the actual circumstances surrounding his death.

Further along the row of headstones is the grave of twenty-nine year old Lieutenant Den Brotheridge (grave 43). To the left of his headstone is:

4) *Memorial Plaque To The First English Soldier Killed At Bénouville (Pegasus) Bridge*. This memorial plaque was donated by the Gondrée family.

Continue along the path until you reach the church tower that is separate from the main church, to your left is the entrance to:

5) *Ranville Church*. It was to be used as an aid

post on 6 June but when Captain David Tibbs, of No. 3 Section 225 Para Fd Amb RAMC, had made his way to the church from the DZ at 0430hrs, he was unable to gain entry. Not yet having any casualties to deal with and content that the field ambulance was being

British 6pdr anti-tank gun awaits the Panzers.

set up he decided they would not need to use the church at that time.

Later the church was turned into an Advanced Dressing Station (ADS). Private Ray Shuck remembers the church well as a result of being taken there for treatment after he was seriously wounded a few days after D-Day. Private Shuck had landed by glider onto DZ N with his section from 4 Airldg A Tk Bty RA at 0330hrs on 6 June.

> *We crashed, but we were lucky as he swerved and he kept the glider level. We managed to get the ramps out and the 6 pdr anti-tank gun and the jeep out with all the ammo in and we weren't far from Ranville and that's where we started to meet opposition. We were to rendezvous at the church, so we fought our way through Ranville and then turned towards the bridges.*
>
> PRIVATE RAY SHUCK, 4 AIRLDG A TK BTY RA,
> ATT 13 PARA, 5 PARA BDE

Private Shuck and the rest of his three man crew, Sergeant Les Marriot and Private Les Atwell, quickly got their 6pdr gun into action. Within a few days Private Shuck's comrade, Private Atwell, had his leg blown off below the knee. Soon after, in action against another German attack, Private Shuck also became a casualty when he was shot by a sniper. As the layer/firer he was moving about near the front gun shield of the gun, raising his

RANVILLE
LE PREMIER VILLAGE DE FRANCE
LIBERE A ETE PRIS AUX ALLEMANDS
A 2ʰ30 LE 6 JUIN 1944
PAR
LE 13ᵀᴴ (LANCASHIRE) BATTALION
THE PARACHUTE REGIMENT

THIS MEMORIAL IS RAISED BY ALL RANKS IN MEMORY
OF THEIR COMRADES WHO FELL IN THE CAMPAIGN

head just a fraction too high on one occasion was enough to present a German sniper with a target. Private Shuck fell to the ground unconscious. As the battle continued he remained unaware until he regained consciousness and found a young boy trying to stop the bleeding from his head.

> *The lad that saved my life, I thought he was a French boy. I found out later he was a Russian living in Ranville and after the war he emigrated to New Zealand. I was twenty at the time this lad was about fifteen. He got me to a French doctor 'cos I was pouring with blood out of my head. I found out later the doctor's name was a Dr Izzard. The doctor and this boy, as some of our troops had advanced by then, they managed, I don't know how and God knows how far it was, they managed to get me back to the church… I can tell exactly where I was laid 'cos I'd come round a bit after blacking out. In that church all the pews and everything were moved out, it was like one big floor. And you know where the pillars are, all down one side. The narrow part of*

Private Ray Shuck (top right) being evacuated after his medical treatment.

one side all the dead were down there, French as well. And the wounded were in the middle. Our medics were treating Germans as well as us. The Germans didn't think that would happen they thought we wouldn't bother, but they were treating them in turn. There was rows and rows of wounded. How the bloody hell they managed, I don't know...My wound put a groove in my skull and the bullet came in and out of my tin hat... But I was fortunate; the surgeon said if it had been any lower it would have blown the back of my head out.

PRIVATE RAY SHUCK, 4 AIRLDG A TK BTY RA,
ATT 13 PARA, 5 PARA BDE

Inside the church in the far right corner is a:

6) 6th Airborne Division Memorial Stained Glass Window. This beautiful window is dedicated to the men of the 6th Airborne Division. Beneath the window on the wall is a white marble:

7) 13 Para Bn Memorial Plaque. Dedicated to 'Luard's Own', after their commanding officer Lieutenant Colonel Peter Luard, and 13 (Lancashire) Para Bn. Left of this there is a brass:

8) Memorial Plaque to Edouard Gérard. This memorial is dedicated to the first Belgian soldier to be killed in Normandy. He was killed in the village of Sallenelles. (see Ch. 7, B1, B18 & Battleground Europe book *Merville Battery & The Dives Bridges* Ch. 5, A2, A3, B5 & D21). His grave is the only Belgian soldier buried in Ranville Commonwealth War Cemetery. Nearby, to your right there is a brass:

9) 1 Cdn Para Memorial Plaque. This memorial is dedicated to the people of Ranville by 1 Cdn Para Bn Association for their friendship and preservation of the graves of the Canadian paratroopers who died in Normandy during 1944.

Return to the main entrance of the churchyard and exit the churchyard via the wrought iron gates. To your right there is a marble plaque on the side of the churchyard wall that names this area:

10) Place Général Sir Richard Gale, named in honour of the CO of the 6th Airborne Division, Major General Richard Gale. Behind you, approximately 75 yards (69m) away on the *Rue Des Airbornes* in the grounds of the *Mairie* (town hall), in front of the

Bibliotheque Municipale (town library), there is a:

11) Bronze Bust of General Richard Gale. This bust, The second of three sculptured by Vivien Mallock (see Ch. 6, A24 & Battleground Europe book *Merville Battery & The Dives Bridges* Ch. 5, D33), is also dedicated to Major General Gale 1896 – 1982, and was presented to the mayor and people of Ranville by the Airborne Assault Normandy Trust in 1994 and unveiled by HRH The Prince of Wales. To the right of the bust on the wall there is:

12) Original 13 (Lancashire) Para Commemorative Plaque. This memorial was originally sited some 260 yards (238m) away farther east along the *Rue des Airbornes* at the junction of the D37 and D223 at *Place du 6 Juin 1944*. This plaque, raised by all ranks of 13 Para in memory of all their comrades who fell, was originally unveiled and dedicated in August 1944. It was later moved to this present location.

Walk out of the *Mairie* grounds and turn left along the *Rue des Airbornes* up towards the *Place du 6 Juin 1944*. Here is sited:

13) New 13 (Lancashire) Para Commemorative Plaque. This new plaque, again in memory of those of 13 Para Bn who fell, was unveiled at this junction on 7 June 1998. If you continue due north-east, across the road from *Place du 6 Juin 1944*, along the D233 for approximately 210 yards (192m) you will come to a road on your left-hand side called:

14) Rue du Général Poett. This road is named in honour of the CO of 5 Para Bde, the then Brigadier Nigel Poett. This was unveiled by Major Simon Poett in memory of his father.

If you continue down *Rue du Général Poett* for about 95 yards (87m) it leads to:

15) Allée Charles Strafford. In honour of Major Charles Strafford (see Ch. 7, B19).

Walk back to *Place du 6 Juin 1944* and back along *Rue des Airbornes*, past the *Mairie*, and turn left at the junction. About 15 yards (13.5m) from the junction, along the footpath, stop at the:

16) OVERLORD l'Assault Marker. This is another of the many markers that covers the route through the Anglo-Canadian Sector (see Ch. 6, A23).

Continue walking along the path until you reach your vehicle. Adjacent to the car park, on your left, there is a wall on which there is a:

17) *Map of 6th Airborne Division's Operations*. Originally drawn by Sapper G.L. Rawlinson of the Royal Engineers this map was presented and unveiled to the people of Ranville in 1981. The map details accounts of the operation and lists the units involved.

Continue to walk along the footpath, across the street, *Rue de la Brigade Piron*, and towards the old mill tower some 32 yards (29m) away. On the blocked up doorway to the tower, facing the cemetery, there is a bronze:

18) *Memorial Plaque to the Belgian Piron Brigade*. This memorial is dedicated to the Belgian combatants who fell in August 1944 and to their comrades in the 6th Airborne Division. *1 Belgian Piron Bde* was placed under the command of the 6th Airborne Division on 8 August, a day after their arrival in Normandy. In the following weeks the brigade would experience some of its action in and around the village of Sallenelles, where one of their youngest members, Edouard Gérard would become the first fatal casualty for the brigade (see Ch. 7, B1, B8 and Battleground Europe book *Merville Battery & The Dives Bridges* Ch. 5, A2, A3, B5 & D21). To the left of the mill tower there is a low stone wall with a marble:

19) *Major Charles Strafford MBE Memorial Plaque*. In memory of Major Strafford who served with General Gale in 6th Airborne Division HQ. After the war he became a summer resident in Ranville until he died in 1993, aged seventy-nine (see Ch. 7, B15 & Battleground Europe book *Merville Battery & The Dives Bridges* Ch. 5, D3). Back around the other side of the mill tower there is a seat bench, facing the cemetery. On the backrest there is a brass:

Edouard Gérard.

20) *Memorial Plaque to the Fallen Scottish Airborne Soldiers*. This seat and plaque was dedicated by Brigadier Alastair Pearson CB DSO MC KSJ TD on 18 October 1994, on behalf of the Central Scotland Branch of the Parachute Regiment Association, in memory of the Scottish airborne soldiers who died in Normandy. The ceremony was also attended by the mayors of Ranville, Troarn, Bures and Touffréville.

Memorial plaque to *Belgian Piron Brigade*.

This concludes your tours around the memorials of 6th Airborne Division in this sector. For a complete tour of the area of operations of the 6th Airborne Division this tour can be continued in Chapter 5 of the Battleground Europe book *Merville Battery & The Dives Bridges*.

APPENDIX A

CHAPTER NOTES AND SOURCES

Chapter One

1. Montgomery, Volume II *Normandy to the Baltic, Invasion*, Corgi Books (1974), p. 231.
2. Report by Dwight D. Eisenhower to Combined Chiefs of Staff (1946), (referred to hereafter as Eisenhower Report) pp. 16, 11, 12 & 15 respectively.
3. Airborne Forces compiled by Lt Col TBH Otway, DSO Imperial War Museum (1990), p. 94. (Referred to hereafter as Otway, Airborne Forces).
4. Gale, *With the 6th Airborne in Normandy*, Sampson Low, Marston & Co. Ltd. (1948), pp. 10-11.
5. ibid., p. 33.
6. Compiled in part from: Facsimile of Major Lacoste's Top Secret intelligence assessment report of 8 May 1944, and a report on the 6th Airborne Division Operations in Normandy June 1944, (compiled for battlefield studies by the Airborne Assault Normandy Trust - referred to hereafter as 'AANT, Battlefield Study').
7. Compiled in part from AANT, Battlefield Study.
8. Saunders, *The Green Beret*, Michael Joseph Ltd. (1949), pp. 261-263.
9. Gale, *With the 6th Airborne in Normandy*, Sampson Low, Marston & Co. Ltd. (1948), p. 50.
10. Harclerode, *'Go To It' The Illustrated History of the 6th Airborne Division*, Bloomsbury, 1990, p. 77.
11. Report On The Operations Carried Out by 6 Airborne Division In Normandy 5 June – 3 Sept 44.
12. Anon., *Part II, The Air Plan*, Staff College Camberley Course Documents (1947).
13. Crookenden, *Dropzone Normandy*, Ian Allen Ltd. (1976). p. 201.
14. Weeks, *Airborne Equipment: A History of its Development*, David & Charles Ltd. (1976). pp. 127, 55, 57 & 58.

Chapter Two

1. Maguire, *Dieppe August 19th 1942*, Jonathan Cape (1963), pp. 183 & 184.
2. Wilmot, *The Struggle for Europe*, Collins (1952). p. 186.
3. ibid., pp. 186 & 187.
4. ibid., p. 199.
5. Eisenhower, *Crusade in Europe*, William Heinemann Ltd (1948). pp. 262-27.

Chapter Three

1. Ambrose, *Pegasus Bridge, 6 June 1944*, George Allen & Unwin (1984), pp 1-13. The details of Private Romer were obtained from a letter Private Romer, then a prisoner of war, had sent to Major Howard.
2. ibid.,
3. Middlebrook & Everitt, *The Bomber Command War Diaries: 1939-1945*, Viking (1985), p. 523.
4. op. cit., Ambrose pp. 2 & 3.
5. Anon., *By Air To Battle: The Official Account of the British Airborne Divisions*, HMSO (1945), p. 77.
6. Howarth, *Dawn of D-Day*, Odhams Press Ltd. (1959). p. 47. & Vaughan, *All Spirits*, Merlin Books Ltd. (1988), pp. 72 & 73.

Chapter Four

1. Compiled from Top Secret Intelligence Report dated 17 May 1944. This report was compiled from RAF reconnaissance missions and details provided by members of the French Resistance.
2. Vaughan, *All Spirits*, Merlin Books Ltd. (1988), p. 75.
3. Anon., *By Air To Battle; The Official Account of the British Airborne Divisions*, HMSO (1945), pp. 77 & 78.
4. op. cit., Ambrose, p. 82.
5. Anon., *By Air To Battle: The Official Account of the British Airborne Divisions*, HMSO (1945), p 78.

Chapter Five

1. ibid., p 79.
2. Anon., *By Air To Battle; The Official Account of the British Airborne Divisions*, HMSO (1945), pp. 79.
3. Vaughan, *All Spirits*, Merlin Books Ltd. (1988). pp. 83 & 84.
4. War Diary entry for 1 SS Bde HQ.
5. McNish, *Iron Division: The History of The 3rd Division*, Ian Allen Ltd. (1978), pp. 99-104.

APPENDIX B

RECOMMENDED READING AND BIBLIOGRAPHY

Recommended Reading

Since the first edition of this work (*Pegasus Bridge & Merville Battery*) was completed in 1999, there have been quite a number of additional works published relating to the 6th Airborne Division in Normandy. In particular, the growth of the internet and world wide web has allowed many documents, articles and photographs to become much more easily available for the battlefield enthusiast and historians alike. Some of those publications are mentioned in the following bibliography; however, a few sources do deserve special mention as they will provide the reader of this work with much extra interesting information about this subject.

Many of the National Archive documents are available for viewing on **www.pegasusarchive.org/normandy/main.htm.** Built and maintained by Mark Hickman. This is undoubtedly one of the most valuable sources regarding information on the 6th Airborne Division that has been made freely available on the web. There is also much additional information as well as many articles, links and photographs available to view.

For information directly from those higher ranking officers who were in Normandy the following are particularly recommended: *Dropzone Normandy* by Napier Crookenden. This covers all the airborne landings in Normandy, and *With The 6th Airborne Division In Normandy* by R.N. Gale, is an account by the commanding officer of the division.

With regards further eyewitness accounts of veterans who served in Normandy; Neil Barber has published his work, *The Pegasus And Orne Bridges*, in 2009. The author has edited many eyewitness accounts together covering the events early in June 1944 and this work will provide the reader with much extra interesting detail of this period (available from **www.pen-and-sword.co.uk**).

For those wishing to know more individual detail about the officers and NCOs who led the 6th Airborne Division, Carl Rijmen (aka Rymen) published his work, *Gale's Eyes*, in 2009. After many years of research he has compiled a list and biographical detail of nearly every officer and NCO who served in the 6th Airborne Division. Although this work is not generally available, a copy of the work, and cost, can be obtained by emailing: **pegasuscr2002@yahoo.com**.

In addition to much correspondence, many interviews and tours around the battlefields with veterans during the last two decades, this work has also been compiled with use of the following documents, publications and articles:

Official Sources
'6 Ab Div Outline Plan Map', Scale 1:25,000, printed by 42 Survey Engineer Group, source AANT.

AANT Battlefield Study, '6th Airborne Division Operations in Normandy June 1944', extracts from PRO docs.

Anon, *By Air To Battle: The Official Account of the British Airborne Divisions*, HMSO (1945).

Anon, 'Report On Operations In Normandy 5 June – 3 Sep 44', compiled from PRO docs, reference unknown.

Lacoste, Major, 'Top Secret intelligence assessment report of 8 May 1944', source and reference unknown.

Report by Dwight D. Eisenhower to Combined Chiefs of Staff, HMSO (1946).

National Archives (formerly Public Record Office)

WO 171/425: 6 Ab Div HQ

WO 171/1242: 9 Para

WO 171/1239: 7 Para

WO 171/1246: 13 Para

WO 171/591: 6 Airldg Bde

WO 171/1018: 2 Airldg Lt AA Bty

WO 171/960: 4 Airldg A Tk Bty

WO 171/2950: 1 Cdn Para

WO 171/595: 5 Para Bde HQ

WO 171/1245: 12 Para

WO 171/1249 22 Ind Para Coy

WO 171/1357: 2 Oxf Bucks

WO 171/959: 3 Airldg A Tk Bty

WO 171/1019: 53 (WY) Airldg Lt Regt

WO 171/1652: 591 Para Sqn RE

WO 171/1622: 286 Fd Pk Coy RE

WO 171/1234: No. 1 Wing Glider Pilot Regt

WO 171/2371: 63 Ab Div Comp Coy RASC

WO 171/2525: 716 Ab Lt Comp Coy RASC

WO 171/433: 6 Ab Div Ord Fd Pk

WO 171/436: 6 Ab Div Pro Coy

WO 171/1605: 249 Fd Coy RE

WO 171/429: 6 Ab Div Sigs

WO 171/1235: No. 2 Wing Glider Pilot Regt

WO 171/2453: 398 Ab Comp Coy RASC

WO 177/793: 195 Airlanding Fd Amb

WO 171/434: 6 Ab Div Ord Fd Pk

WO 218/59: 1 SS Bde HQ

Publications
Titles in bold are written by, or diaries of, veterans of the campaign

Ambrose, Stephen, *Pegasus Bridge, 6 June 1944*, George Allen & Unwin (1984).

Arthur, Max, *Men of The Red Beret*, Hutchinson (1992).

Bailey, Roderick, *Forgotten Voices of D-Day*, Edbury Press (2009).

Barber, Neil, *The Pegasus and Orne Bridges*, Pen & Sword Books Ltd. (2009).

Barley, Eric & Fohlen, Yves, *Para Memories: 12 (Yorkshire) Para Bn*, Parapress Ltd. (1996).

Bellis, Malcolm A, *Regiments of The British Army 1939-45 (Artillery)*, Military Press International (1995).

Bernage, Georges, *Red Devils in Normandy*, Heimdal (2002).

Bowman, Martin W., *Remembering D-Day*, Harper Collins Pub. (2004).

Chant, Christopher, *Order of Battle: Operation Overlord*, vol. I, Ravelin Ltd.(1994).

Chatterton, George, *The Wings of Pegasus*, Macdonald (1962).

Collier, Richard, *Ten Thousand Eyes*, Collins (1958).

Crookenden, Napier, *Dropzone Normandy*, Ian Allen Ltd. (1976).

Davies, Howard P., *British Parachute Forces 1940-45*, Arms & Armour Press (1974).

Delve, Ken, *D-DAY The Air Battle*, The Crowood Press (2004).

Doherty, Richard, *Normandy 1944*, Spellmount (2004).

Dover, Major Victor, *The Sky Generals*, Cassell Ltd. (1981).

Durnford-Slater, Brig John, *Commando*, William Kimber & Co. Ltd. (1953).

Edwards, Denis, *The Devil's Own Luck*, Pen & Sword Books Ltd. (1999).

Edwards, Commander Kenneth, *Operation Neptune*, Collins (1946).

Eisenhower, Gen Dwight D., *Crusade in Europe*, William Heinemann Ltd. (1948).

Ellis, Major L.F., *Victory in The West*, vol. I, HMSO (1962).

Ford, Ken, *D-Day 1944 (3) Sword Beach & British Airborne Landings,*
Osprey Publishing (2002).

Gale, R. N., *A Call To Arms*, Hutchinson (1968).

Gale, R.N., *With The 6th Airborne Division in Normandy*, Sampson, Low & Marston (1948).

Gregory, Barry & John Batchelor, *Airborne Warfare 1918-1945*, Phoebus Publishing Co. (1979)

Harclerode, Peter, *Go To It!*, Bloomsbury (1990).

Harclerode, Peter, *Para*, Arms & Armour Press (1992).

Hargreaves, Richard, *The Germans in Normandy*, Pen & Sword Books Ltd. (2006).

Hastings, Max, *Overlord*, Michael Joseph Ltd. (1984).

Hogg, Ian V. (Intro.), *German Order of Battle 1944*, Arms & Armour Press (1975).

Holt, Major & Mrs, *Normandy D-Day Landing Beaches*, Pen & Sword Books Ltd. (1999 & 2006).

Howard, John & Bates, P., ***The Pegasus Journals***, **Pen & Sword Books Ltd. (2006).**

Howarth, David, *Dawn of D-Day*, Chivers Press (1959).

Isby, David C. (Ed.), *Fighting The Invasion: The German Army At D-Day*, Greenhill Books (2000).

Leeming, Raymond, *And Maybe A Man: With The Royal Signals Of 6 Ab Div*, Parapress Ltd. (1995).

Johnson, Garry & Christopher Dunphie, *Brightly Shone The Dawn*, Frederick Warne (1980).

Lynch, Tim, *Silent Skies*, Pen & Sword Books Ltd. (2008).

Maguire, Eric, *Dieppe August 19th 1942*, Jonathan Cape (1963).

McNish, Robin, *Iron Division*, Ian Allen Ltd. (1978).

Middlebrook & Everitt, *The Bomber Command War Diaries: 1939-1945*, Viking (1985).

Montgomery, *Normandy to the Baltic, Invasion*, vol. II, Hutchinson & Co. Ltd. (1947).

Neillands, Robin, *The Raiders: The Army Commandos*, Weidenfeld & Nicolson Ltd. (1989).

Norton, G.G., *The Red Devils*, Leo Cooper (1971).

NVA, Members of Dorset 84 Branch, *Memories of World War II*, Private Publication (2002).

NVA, Members of South East 23 Branch, *Memories of Normandy 1944*, Private Publication (2005).

Otway, T., *Airborne Forces*, Imperial War Museum (1990).

Pine-Coffin, P & B. Maddox, *The Tale Of Two Bridges*, Private Publication (2004).

Poett, N., *Pure Poett*, Leo Cooper (1991).

Ramsey, Winston G. (ed.), *Normandy After The Battle*, vol, I, After The Battle (1977).

Rijmen, Carl, *Gale's Eyes: 6 Ab Div Who Was Who in Normandy*, Private Pub (2009).

Robins, Bernard & Fay, *Remembered With Honour: 8 Para*, Private Publication (2002).

Saunders, Hilary St George, *The Green Beret*, Michael Joseph Ltd. (1949).

Saunders, Hilary St George, *The Red Beret*, Michael Joseph Ltd. (1950).

Scarfe, Norman, *Assault Division*, Collins (1947).

Shannon, K. & Wright, S., *One Night in June*, Airlife Publishing Ltd. (1994).

Shave, Major J.S.R., *Go To It: The Story of the 3rd Parachute Squadron RE* (2003).

Shaw, F. & Shaw, J., *We Remember D-Day*, Private Publication (1983).

Shilleto, Carl, *Fallen Heroes of Normandy 1944: The Commonwealth War Cemeteries*, Pen & Sword Books Ltd. (2012).

Shilleto, Carl, *Pegasus Bridge Merville Battery*, Pen & Sword Books Ltd. (1999).

Shilleto, Carl, *The D-Day Beaches of Normandy*, Leger (1999).

Shilleto, Carl & Mike Tolhurst *The Traveller's Guide to D-Day and The Battle For Normandy*, Interlink Pub. (2000).

Smith, Claude, *The History of The Glider Pilot Regiment*, Leo Cooper (1992)

Thompson, Major General Julian, *Ready For Anything*, Weidenfield & Nicolson Ltd. (1989).

Todd, Richard, *Caught in the Act*, Hutchinson (1987).

Tugwell, Maurice, *Airborne to Battle*, William Kimber, (1971).

Vaughan, John, *All Spirits*, Merlin Books Ltd, (1988).

Weeks, John, *Airborne Equipment. A History of its Development*, David & Charles Ltd. (1976).

Weeks, John, *Assault From The Sky*, Westbridge Books (1978).

Wheldon, Sir Huw, *Red Berets into Normandy*, Jarrold & Sons Ltd. (1982).

Wilmot, Chester, *Struggle For Europe*, Collins (1952).

Wilson, Chris & Col John Nowers, *D-Day June 1944 And The Engineers*, Royal Engineers Museum (1994).

Wynn, Humphrey & Susan Young, *Prelude To Overlord*, Airlife (1983).

Young, Brigadier Peter, *Storm From The Sea*, Greenhill Books (2002).

Zetterling, Niklas, *Normandy 1944: German Military Effectiveness*, J.J. Fedorowicz Pub Inc. (2000).

Articles & Papers

Anon., '6th Airborne Division Roll of Honour 1944-45', pp. 1-44, source unknown (no date).

Anon., 'The Register Of The Graves (6 AB Div)', pp. 1-25, Source unknown – prob. CWGC – (no date).

Anon., 'Part II, The Air Plan', Staff College Camberley Course Documents (1947).

Buck, Captain T.G., 'Ham & Jam Battlefield Tour 1996', *The Bucks Bugle*, pp. 1-36, (1996).

Lowman, Brigadier F.H., 'The 6th Ab Div Engineers on D-Day 1944', *Corps History.* Vol IX, pp. 339-343, (no date).

Plaice, Ellis, various articles, *Red Berets '44, The London Illustrated News'*, pp. 3-65, (1994).

Useful Websites

Archives & Research (British, Canadian & French Forces)

www.nationalarchives.gov.uk

www.cwgc.org

www.pegasusarchive.org/normandy/frames

www.1940.co.uk/history/article/merville/merville.htm

www.6commando.com

www.6juin1944.com/en_index.html

www.bayonetstrength.150m.com/British/Airborne/british_parachute_battalion%201944%20to%201945.htm

www.britisharmedforces.org

www.britisharmedforces.org/pages/nat_jim_wallwork.htm

www.britisharmedforces.org/pages/nat_richard_todd.htm

www.combinedops.com/Combined_Ops_index.htm

www.gliderpilotregiment.org.uk

www.gotoitgunners.co.uk

www.normandy1944.info

www.normandie44lamemoire.com/versionanglaise/indexus.html

www.paradata.org.uk/events/normandy-operation-overlord

www.prinsesirenebrigade.nl/

www.raf38group.org

www.theairbornesoldier.com

www.trueloyals.com

www.ww2battlefields.com

Archives & Research (German Forces)

www.atlantikwall.co.uk

www.axishistory.com

British Library

http://portico.bl.uk/

Archive Film

www.britishpathe.com/results.php?search=Normandy+1944&o=0

Pegasus Journal

www.army.mod.uk/infantry/regiments/5904.aspx

Museums (France)

www.batterie-merville.com/index_uk.html

www.the-snafu-special.com

www.junobeach.org/e/4/can-tac-par-e.htm

www.musee-4commando.org/1st_bfmc_120.htm

www.memorialpegasus.org/mmp/musee_debarquement/index.php?lang=uk

Museums (UK)

www.airborneassault.org.uk

www.ddaymuseum.co.uk

www.d-daytanks.org.uk/regiments/6th-airborne.html

www.flying-museum.org.uk

www.iwm.org.uk

www.remuseum.org.uk/campaign/rem_campaign_6adiv.htm

Airborne Engineers Association

www.airbornesappers.org.uk

Commando Veterans Association

www.commandoveterans.org/site

Normandy Veterans Association

www.nvafriends.nl/index.php?cid=36

The Parachute Regimental Association

www.army.mod.uk/infantry/regiments/5905.aspx

The Royal British Legion

www.poppy.org.uk

Airborne Charities and Projects

www.abfc.org.uk

www.airborneforcesmemorial.org.uk

www.army.mod.uk/infantry/regiments/4795.aspx

www.assaultgliderproject.co.uk

www.fallenheroesphotos.org

www.project65.net

www.sopara.org.uk

Living History Groups

www.1canpara.com/

www.1canpara-hq.org
www.6th-airborne.org
www.7thpara.netfirms.com

Research Services
www.findasoldier.co.uk
www.ww2battlefields.com/ww2_research.htm

Forums
http://forum.axishistory.com/
www.ww2talk.com

Battlefield Tours
www.ddayhistorian.com
www.guidedbattlefieldtours.co.uk
www.leger.co.uk
www.normandybattletours.com

APPENDIX C
ORDER OF BATTLE
6th Airborne Division, Normandy Landings
6 June, 1944

Divisional Headquarters

GOC	..	..	..	Maj Gen Richard Gale
ADC	..	..	..	Captain Tom Haughton
AA & QMG	..	..	..	Lt Col Shamus Hickie
ADMS	..	..	..	Lt Col M. MacEwan
GSO 1 (Air)	..	..	..	Lt Col W. Bradish
GSO 1 (Ops)	..	..	..	Lt Col Bobby Bray
GSO 2 (Ops)	..	..	..	Major David Baird
GSO 2 (Int)	..	..	..	Major Gerry Lacoste
GSO 3 (Ops)	..	..	..	Captain M. Spurling
GSO 3 (Int)	..	..	..	Captain J. Max
GSO 3 (Air)	..	..	..	Captain Nick Pratt

3rd Parachute Brigade

Commander	..	..	..	Brig James Hill
1 Cdn Para Bn	..	..	..	Lt Col George Bradbrooke
8 Para Bn		..	..	Lt Col Alastair Pearson
9 Para Bn		..	..	Lt Col Terence Otway

5th Parachute Brigade

Commander	..	..	..	Brig Nigel Poett
7 Para Bn		..	..	Lt Col Richard G. Pine-Coffin
12 Para Bn	..	..	..	Lt Col Johnny Johnson
13 Para Bn	..	..	..	Lt Col Peter Luard

22nd (Independent) Parachute Company (Pathfinders)

Commander	..	..	..	Major Francis Lennox-Boyd

6th Airlanding Brigade

Commander	..	..	..	Brig Hon Hugh Kindersley
Deputy	..	..	..	Colonel Reggie Parker
1 RUR	..	..	..	Lt Col R. Carson
2 Oxf Bucks	..	..	..	Lt Col Michael Roberts
12 Devons	..	..	..	Lt Col Dick Stevens

Royal Armoured Corps

6 AARR		..	..	Lt Col Godfrey Stewart

Royal Artillery

CRA	..	..	..	Lt Col Jack Norris
2 Airldg Lt AA Bty	..	..	Major W. Rowat
2 Forward Observer Unit	..	Major Harry Rice
3 Airldg A Tk Bty	..	..	Major W. Cranmer
4 Airldg A Tk Bty	..	..	Major T. Dixon
53 (WY) Airldg Lt Regt....	..	Lt Col Tony Teacher
210 Airldg Lt Bty	..	..	Major Hon C. Russell
211 Airldg Lt Bty	..	..	Major Tim Craigie
212 Airldg Lt Regt	..	..	Major Matt Gubbins

Royal Engineers

CRE .. .. .. Lt Col Frank Lowman
3 Para Sqn RE .. .. .. Major Tim Roseveare
591 Para Sqn RE .. .. Major P. Wood
249 Fd Coy RE .. .. .. Major A. Rutherford
286 Fd Pk Coy RE .. .. Major Jack Waters

Royal Signals

6 Ab Div Sigs .. .. .. Lt Col D. Smallman-Tew

Army Air Corps

No.1 Wing Glider Pilot Regt .. Lt Col I. Murray
No.2 Wing Glider Pilot Regt .. Lt Col P. Griffiths

Royal Army Service Corps

CRASC .. .. .. Lt Col J. Watson
63 Ab Div Comp Coy .. .. Major A. Bille-Top
398 Ab Comp Coy .. .. Major M. Phipps
716 Ab Lt Comp Coy .. .. Major A. Jones.

Royal Army Medical Corps

195 Airlanding Fd Amb .. .. Lt Col Bill Anderson
224 Para Fd Amb .. .. Lt Col D. H. Thompson
225 Para Fd Amb .. .. Lt Col Bruce Harvey

Royal Army Ordnance Corps

6 Ab Div Ord Fd Pk .. Major W.L. Taylor

Royal Electrical and Mechanical Engineers

CREME .. .. .. Lt Col R. Powditch
6 Airborne Div Wkshop.. .. Major E. Bonniwell
9 Airldg LAD .. .. .. ——————
10 Airldg LAD .. .. .. ——————
12 Airldg LAD .. .. .. ——————

Royal Corps of Military Police

6 Ab Div Pro Coy, Commander		Captain Irwin
245 HQ Pro Coy	.. ..	————————

Royal Army Intelligence Corps

317 Fd Security Sec   ..   ..   Captain F.G. Macmillan

Under Command of 6th Airborne Division during Campaign

1 Special Service Brigade

Commander	Brig The Lord Lovat
3 Commando	Lt Col Peter Young
4 Commando*	Lt Col Robert Dawson
6 Commando	Lt Col Derek Mills-Roberts
45 (Royal Marine) Cdo	Lt Col Charles Ries
1 *BMFC*, No 1 & No 8 Tp, 10 (IA) Cdo*	*Commandant* Philippe Keiffer

* Under Command of 3rd Infantry Division

4 Special Service Brigade

Commander	Brig B.W. Leicester
41 (Royal Marine) Cdo	Lt Col E. Palmer
46 (Royal Marine) Cdo	Lt Col C.R. Hardy
47 (Royal Marine) Cdo	Lt Col C.F. Phillips
48 (Royal Marine) Cdo	Lt Col J.C. Moulton

Princess Irene Brigade	*Lt Kol Arty* A. C. de Ruyter van Steveninck
1 Belgian Piron Brigade	*Colonel* Jean Piron

APPENDIX D

The Satellite Navigation coordinates (Google Earth) are listed below for all main locations. Some of the memorials, exhibits or headstones are not listed individually as these can be found in close proximity to the location and because some memorial seat bench plaques and exhibits are periodically relocated, but remain in the same general area.

All coordinates are given in Degrees, Minutes and Seconds. Additional information and photographs of the memorials, exhibits and locations can be viewed at www.earth.google.com (NB. you may need to activate the appropriate layer).

CHAPTER SIX

A. Pegasus Bridge & Horsa Bridge

1) *Pegasus Bridge signpost*
lat: 49,14,32.83N *long*: 00,16,29.37W

2) *Café Gondrée*
lat: 49,14,32.70N *long*: 00,16,29.80W

3) *First Liberated House in France*
lat: 49,14,32.76N *long*: 00,16,29.78W

4) *7 Para Plaque*
lat: 49,14,32.76N *long*: 00,16,29.78W

5) *Aid Post Plaque*
lat: 49,14,32.76N *long*: 00,16,29.78W

6) *No. 1 Special Service Bde Memorial*
lat: 49,14,32.76N *long*: 00,16,30.45W

7) *Café Gondrée Annexe*
lat: 49,14,31.90N *long*: 00,16,31.03W

8) *Pegasus Bridge Café Gondrée Signpost*
lat: 49,14,33.16N *long*: 00,16,30.90W

9) *First Bailey Bridge Memorial Plaque*
lat: 49,14,17.89N *long*: 00,16,41.66W

10) *Bénouville Château*
lat: 49,14,10.75N *long*: 00,16,52.50W

11) *Airborne and Commando Memorial Marker*
lat: 49,14,33.48N *long*: 00,16,31.54W
12) *Bénouville Mairie*
lat: 49,14,35.40N *long*: 00,16,41.20W
13) *First World War Memorial*
lat: 49,14,35.97N *long*: 00,16,40.89W
14) *7 Para Bn Memorial*
lat: 49,14,37.18N *long*: 00,16,40.47W
15) *Bénouville Church and Churchyard*
lat: 49,14,48.10N *long*: 00,16,34.05W
16) *Les 3 Planeurs*
lat: 49,14,34.51N *long*: 00,16,29.80W
17) *Centaur IV (A27L) Tank*
lat: 49,14,33.79N *long*: 00,16,29.33W
18) *2 Oxf Bucks Commemoration Plaque.*
lat: 49,14,32.00N *long*: 00,16,25.95W

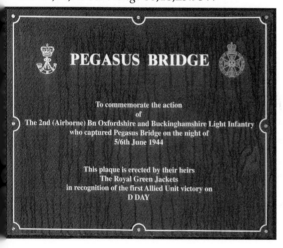

19) *Esplanade John Howard*
lat: 49,14,31.25N *long*: 00,16,25.47W
20) *50mm (1.97in) Kwk Anti-Tank Gun.*
lat: 49,14,31.56N *long*: 00,16,25.65W
21) *Comité du Débarquement Monument*
lat: 49,14,30.77N *long*: 00,16,25.59W
22) *'The Pegasus Trail' Orientation Table (1)*
lat: 49,14,30.27N *long*: 00,16,25.80W
23) *OVERLORD l'Assault Marker*
lat: 49,14,30.95N *long*: 00,16,24.95W

24) *Bronze Bust of Major John Howard*
lat: 49,14,29.81N *long*: 00,16,24.95W
25) *First Glider Landing Marker*
lat: 49,14,29.89N *long*: 00,16,24.89W
26) *Third Gilder Landing Marker*
lat: 49,14,28.46N *long*: 00,16,24.65W

27) *Second Glider Landing Marker*
lat: 49,14,27.42N *long*: 00,16,23.75W
28) *Horsa Bridge*
lat: 49,14,25.07N *long*: 00,16,00.61W
29) *Bridge Support Remains*
lat: 49,14,21.78N *long*: 00,16,01.40W
30) *Horsa Bridge Memorial*
lat: 49,14,25.82N *long*: 00,16,02.54W

B. Memorial Pegasus Museum *(Musée Mémorial Pegasus)*
lat: 49,14,32.40N *long*: 00,16,18.00W
1) *12 Para Memorial Plaque*
2) *6th Airborne Division Plaque*
3) *5.5in (139.7mm) Medium Gun*
lat: 49,14,33.22N *long*: 00,16,18.62W
4) *6th Airborne Division Memorial Plaque*
5) *3 Para Bde Memorial Plaque*
6) *Brigadier James Hill DSO MC Bronze*
lat: 49,14,33.87N *long*: 00,16,18.34W
7) *2 Oxf Bucks Memorial Plaque*
8) *Memorial to Lieutenant H.D. Brotheridge*
lat: 49,14,34.13N *long*: 00,16,17.97W

9) 25pdr Field Gun
lat: 49,14,34.34N *long*: 00,16,18.14W

10) RAF Memorial Plaque
11) Pegasus Bridge Signpost
lat: 49,14,34.68N *long*: 00,16,17.75W
12) 8 Para Battalion Memorial Plaque
13) Lt Gen Sir Napier Crookenden Memorial Plaque
14) Replica Airspeed (AS) 51 Horsa Mk I Glider
lat: 49,14,35.46N *long*: 00,16,16.78W

15) Memorial Plaque to Tom Packwood
16) Sergeant Ken J. Henesey Memorial Plaque
17) Original Horsa Glider Fuselage Section

171

lat: 49,14,35.76N *long*: 00,16,15.73W
18) *Memorial Plaque to Cpl Ted Tappenden*
19) *Royal Engineers Memorial Plaque*
20) *Original Section of Bailey Bridge*
lat: 49,14,34.90N *long*: 00,16,15.60W
21) *13 (Lancashire) Para Memorial Plaque*
22) *2 (Airldg) Oxf Bucks Memorial Plaque*
23) *The Men in Gliders Memorial*
lat: 49,14,34.70N *long*: 00,16,16.30W
24) *Original Pegasus Bridge*
lat: 49,14,34.10N *long*: 00,16,16.80W
25) *Pegasus Bridge Memorial*
26) *40mm (1.58in) Bofors Anti-Aircraft Gun*
lat: 49,14,33.28N *long*: 00,16,16.49W
27) *1 RUR Memorial Plaque*
28) *Quadruple 12.7mm (0.50in) Anti-Aircraft Gun Mounting*
lat: 49,13,32.87N *long*: 00,16,16.51W
29) *M3 A1 Half-Track*
lat: 49,14,32.76N *long*: 00,16,16.74W
30) *RAMC Memorial Plaque*
31) *1 Cdn Para Memorial Plaque*

CHAPTER SEVEN
A. DZ/LZ N (North) & 'The Pegasus Trail' Orientation Table (2
lat: 49,14,24.47N *long*: 00,15,18.36W

B. Ranville
1) *Ranville Commonwealth War Cemetery*
lat: 49,13,52.04N *long*: 00,15,28.15W
2) *Memorial Cross to the 6th Airborne Division*
lat: 49,13,51.28N *long*: 00,15,30.58W

3) *Ranville Churchyard*
lat: 49,13,53.81N *long*: 00,15,29.78W
4) *Memorial Plaque to First Soldier Killed at Pegasus Bridge*
lat: 49,13,56.83N *long*: 00,15,30.38W
5) *Ranville Church*
lat: 49,13,55.70N *long*: 00,15,30.00W

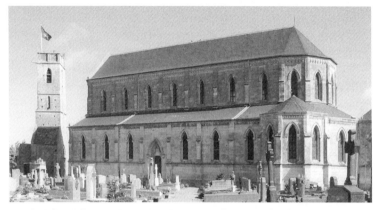

6) *6th Airborne Division Memorial Stained Glass Window*
lat: 49,13,55.22N *long*: 00,15,29.52W
7) *13 Para Bn Memorial Plaque*
lat: 49,13,55.22N *long*: 00,15,29.52W
8) *Memorial Plaque to Edouard Gérard*
lat: 49,13,55.22N *long*: 00,15,29.52W
9) *1 Cdn Para Memorial Plaque*
lat: 49,13,55.22N *long*: 00,15,29.52W
10) *Place General Sir Richard Gale*
lat: 49,13,54.40N *long*: 00,15,28.15W
11) *Bronze Bust of Général Richard Gale*
lat: 49,13,54.85N *long*: 00,15,24.77W
12) *Original 13 (Lancashire) Para Commemorative Plaque*
lat: 49,13,54.81N *long*: 00,15,24.68W

13) *New 13 (Lancashire) Para Commemorative Plaque*
lat: 49,13,51.26N *long*: 00,15,14.38W
14) *Rue du Général Poett*
lat: 49,13,55.76N *long*: 00,15,07.68W
15) *Allée Charles Strafford*
lat: 49,13,57.93N *long*: 00,15,11.15W
16) *OVERLORD l'Assault Marker*
lat: 49,13,54.02N *long*: 00,15,27.34W
17) *Map of 6th Airborne Division's Operations*
lat: 49,13,52.67N *long*: 00,15,27.00W
18) *Memorial Plaque to the Belgian Piron Brigade*
lat: 49,13,51.62N *long*: 00,15,27.42W

19) *Major Charles Strafford MBE Memorial Plaque*
lat: 49,13,51.62N *long*: 00,15,26.74W
20) *Fallen Scottish Airborne Soldiers Memorial Plaque*
lat: 49,13,51.05N *long*: 00,15,27.04W

APPENDIX E

FALLEN HEROES PROJECT, MEMORIAL PEGASUS, CWGC & AANT

FALLEN HEROES OF NORMANDY PROJECT
THE COMMONWEALTH WAR CEMETERIES
A PHOTOGRAPHIC REMEMBRANCE

AN APPEAL FOR PHOTOGRAPHS OF OR INFORMATION ABOUT
THE SERVICEMEN (of all nationalities)
WHO NOW REST IN THE COMMONWEALTH CEMETERIES
OR FRENCH CHURCHYARDS OF NORMANDY

Brothers Cyril and Stan Eckert, killed Normandy 1944. Reproduced by kind permission of Eckert family.

The aim of the project is to compile a detailed record of photographs of individuals and information of those whose graves are now maintained by the Commonwealth War Graves Commission, in Normandy.

The project archives are to be presented to the Commonwealth War Graves Commission in 2017 for their Centenary year and will be made accessible, online, for future generations.

Please email information and scanned photographs (with a resolution of 300 dpi) to:

fallenheroes@btinternet.com

or post* photographs or information to:

Carl Shilleto, Military Historian
c/o The Regimental Museum,
3 Tower Street, York YO1 9SB UK

Photographs of individuals are most sought after, followed by photographs of the previous cross markers or the cemeteries, churchyards or areas as they were in the 1940s. Photographs of present day headstones are no longer required. All correspondence will be acknowledged by email (Please provide email address and allow up to 12 weeks for a reply). This project is not for profit.

Visit: www.fallenheroesphotos.org

Please note that ONLY COPIES of photographs and documents should be sent as we are unable to return any material donated.

SUPPORTED BY

www.cwgc.org   www.battlefields.leger.co.uk   www.pen-and-sword.co.uk   www.awol-yorkshire.museum

Memorial Pegasus Museum (Musée Mémorial Pegasus)
Inaugurated on 4 June 2000 by HRH The Prince of Wales, the Memorial Pegasus is dedicated to the men of the 6th Airborne Division and their role during the Battle of Normandy.

The museum was built, with the help and assistance of the Airborne Assault Normandy Trust, by the D-Day Commemoration Committee. The collection, on display in the museum and memorial garden, is both historically unique and important, situated as it is, on the battlefield itself.

If any veterans of the 6th Airborne Division, their families or friends, are able to donate any items relating to the battles in Normandy, such donations will be gratefully received, acknowledged, catalogued and preserved for posterity within the museum collection.

For further information and details of how to donate any personal items, please contact:
Curator, Mark Worthington, Memorial Pegasus, Avenue du Major Howard 14860 Ranville, France. Tel: 0033 231781944, Fax 0033 231781942, email: info@memorial-pegasus.

The Commonwealth War Graves Commission
Established in May 1917 by Royal Charter, the Commonwealth War Graves Commission is dedicated to marking and maintaining the graves of all those who were killed in the two World Wars, from the forces of the Commonwealth. The cost of this work is shared between Australia, Britain, Canada, India, New Zealand and South Africa in proportion to the number of graves each country has. There are 23,260 burial grounds in 149 countries with a total of 1,694,988 names commemorated. From the Second World War 347,410 graves have been identified, while a further 23,479 remain unidentified. In addition 231,893 people have no known grave and are commemorated on memorials. The Head Office is at: 2 Marlow Road, Maidenhead, Berkshire, SL6 7DX. Tel: 01628 634 221. There is also an internet web site: **www.cwgc.org**. A short guide of the Cemeteries in Normandy can be downloaded from their website.

The Airborne Assault Normandy Trust
As mentioned in the introduction, the AANT was established to help preserve the history and memory of the 6th Airborne Division in Normandy.

Donations, made payable to **The Airborne Assault Normandy Trust**, will be acknowledged, can be forwarded to: Airborne Assault Normandy, Browning Barracks, Aldershot, Hampshire GU11 2BU.

176

APPENDIX F

THE MEN IN GLIDERS

On the night of 5/6th June 1944, of the 704 glider pilots in 352 gliders accounted for in operational records, thirty-two lost their lives on D-Day. At least ten were killed in crash landings, and up to twelve, soon after landing, from enemy fire. Six, along with their passengers, perished in the cold waters of the English Channel and four by direct hits from German anti-aircraft fire. Many were also wounded or injured as a result of enemy fire or unfortunate landings. At least four gliders hit trees and anti-aircraft poles causing broken limbs for at least one of the two pilots.

In one instance Staff Sergeant A.T. Stear was killed on landing after their glider, destined for DZ N, hit a farm building. His co-pilot, Sgt J. Wilson, lay trapped in the glider, next to his dead comrade, for two days until rescued. His injuries were so severe that one of his legs had to be amputated. In another landing, a glider, piloted by Staff Sergeant H.A. Rancom and Sgt E. Collard, came to rest in a minefield. Both survived, but despite trying to hide from the Germans, both were captured by SS troops and made prisoners of war. Staff Sergeant Rancom had his arm amputated. A further fourteen glider pilots were captured by the Germans. Two managed to escape but six would later die in captivity. Among the many others injured during D-Day were pilot Staff Sergeant K.A. Evans and David Woodward, the war correspondent for the *Manchester Guardian*. Their glider, destined for LZ N, crash landed near their target carrying their cargo of a bulldozer for the Royal Engineers. Their co-pilot, Sgt J. Thompson, was later wounded. A further seven glider pilots would die in Normandy during the fighting in the following days.

But for those brave pilots that survived the horrors of Normandy, there would be further operations where they would be needed to carry men and equipment into the battlefields of north-west Europe. On 17 September 1944 Operation MARKET began the race to cross the River Rhine. In that assault, and the action that followed, of the 220 glider pilots who lost their lives eighty-three had previously survived Normandy. Six months later in Operation VARSITY, beginning 23 March 1945, six more veterans of Normandy lost their lives.

Jimmy Edwards.

Of the glider pilots who survived Normandy, one would go on to become an international comedian, stage and film star. Staff Sergeant Jimmy Edwards received a facial wound at Arnhem when his aircraft was shot down. After receiving plastic surgery and becoming a member of the famous Guinea Pig Club, he grew his distinctive handle-bar moustache, which would become his trademark, to hide his wound. Many awards and honours were also bestowed upon glider pilots for action in Normandy including: one AFC, five *Croix de Geurre*, one DCM, three DFCs, eleven DFMs, one DSO, three MIDs and one MM.

This book has concentrated mainly on the experiences of just six of those gliders that landed, in Normandy, on D-Day. Over the years, numerous lists have been compiled and published detailing those men involved in the *Coup de Main* operation to take the bridges over the Caen Canal and River Orne. Initially, there was the official operational list followed by lists compiled by veterans Major John Howard, Private Denis Edwards, Corporal Ted Tappenden and Staff Sergeant Jim Wallwork. In 2009, the most recent and comprehensive list was completed by the founder, members and trustees of Project 65 (www.project65.net).

Pegasus Bridge & Horsa Bridge *Coup de main* parties

Over three years, Mr Barry Tappenden, General Sir Robert Pascoe KCB MBE, Major Michael Massy-Beresford and Mr Danny Greeno, compiled the most definitive list after consulting previous lists and interviewing veterans to try and establish if any men were added or taken off the flight roster before embarkation on 5 June 1944. The resulting list was then used for The Men in Gliders Memorial at the Memorial Pegasus Museum (Musée Mémorial Pegasus (see Ch. 6, B23). Additional information included on the following list has been collated from various sources mentioned in the bibliography.

Glider No. 1 (667),
Chalk mark No. 91,
Serial No. PF800

Glider Pilot Regiment: S/Sgt Wallwork, S/Sgt Ainsworth.

D Coy HQ: Maj Howard (Commanding Officer), Cpl Tappenden (Wireless Operator).

No. 25 Pl D Coy 2 Oxf Bucks: Lt Brotheridge (Platoon Commander), Sgt Ollis, Cpl Bailey, Cpl Caine, Cpl Webb, L/Cpl Minns, L/Cpl Packwood, Pte Baalham, Pte Bates, Pte Bourlet, Pte Chamberlain, Pte Edwards, Pte Gardner, Pte Gray, Pte Jackson 08, Pte O'Donnell, Pte Parr, Pte Tilbury, Pte Watson, Pte White, Pte Windsor.

No. 2 Pl 249 Fd Coy RE: Cpl Watson, Spr Danson, Spr Ramsey, Spr Wheeler, Spr Yates.

Tug: Halifax bomber, LL355-G.

298 Sqn 38 Group RAF: W/C Duder DSO DFC, P/O Mclaren, Sgt Lappin, F/L Palmby, F/S Newling, Sgt McAllum.

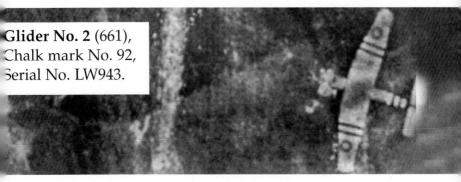

Glider No. 2 (661),
Chalk mark No. 92,
Serial No. LW943.

Glider Pilot Regiment: S/Sgt Boland, S/Sgt Hobbs.

No. 24 Pl D Coy 2 Oxf Bucks: Lt Wood (Platoon Commander), Sgt Leather, Cpl Cowperthwaite, Cpl Godbold, Cpl Ilsley, L/Cpl Drew, L/Cpl Roberts, Pte Chatfield, Pte Cheesley, Pte Clark 48, Pte Clarke 33, Pte Dancey, Pte Harmen, Pte Leonard, Pte Lewis, Pte Malpas, Pte Musty, Pte Pepperall, Pte Radford, Pte Warmington, Pte Waters, Pte Weaver.

RAMC: L/Cpl Harris.

No. 2 Pl 249 Fd Coy RE: Capt Neilson, Spr Conley, Spr Haslett, Spr Lockhart, Spr Shorey.

Tug: Halifax bomber, LL335-K.

298 Sqn 38 Group RAF: W/O Berry, F/S Roberts, P/O Letts, F/S White (RCAF), Sgt Stewart, Sgt Austin (RNAF), F/L Reevely.

Glider No. 3 (663),
Chalk mark No. 93,
Serial No. LH469

Glider Pilot Regiment: S/Sgt Barkway, S/Sgt Boyle.

No. 14 Pl B Coy 2 Oxf Bucks: Lt Smith (Platoon Commander), Sgt Harrison, Cpl Ariss, Cpl Evans, Cpl Higgs, L/Cpl Cohen, L/Cpl Greenhalgh, L/Cpl Madge, Pte Anton, Pte Basham, Pte Burns, Pte Crocker, Pte Golden, Pte Hook, Pte Keane, Pte Noble, Pte Slade, Pte Stewart, Pte Tibbs, Pte Turner, Pte Watts, Pte Wilson.

RAMC: Captain Jacob (aka Vaughan).

No. 2 Pl 249 Fd Coy RE: L/Cpl Waring, Spr Clarke, Spr Fleming, Spr Green, Spr Preece.

Tug: Halifax bomber, LL218-N.

644 Sqn 38 Group RAF: W/O Herman, F/S Mills, Sgt Duncan, F/S Morrison, F/S Walsh, Sgt Waterfall.

Glider No. 4 (662),
Chalk mark No. 94,
Serial No. PF723

Glider Pilot Regiment: S/Sgt Lawrence, S/Sgt Shorter.
D Coy HQ: Capt Priday (2 i/c), L/Cpl Lambley.
No. 22 Pl D Coy 2 Oxf Bucks: Lt Hooper (Platoon Commander), Sgt Barwick, L/Sgt Rayner, Cpl Bateman, Cpl Goodsir, L/Cpl Ambrose, L/Cpl Hunt, Pte Allwood, Pte Clive, Pte Everett, Pte Gardner 08, Pte Hammond, Pte Hedges, Pte Jeffries, Pte Johnson, Pte Lathbury, Pte St Clair, Pte Timms, Pte Waite, Pte Whitford, Pte Wilson.
No. 2 Pl 249 Fd Coy RE: L/Sgt Brown, Spr Deighan, Spr Guest, Spr Paget, Spr Roberts.
Tug: Halifax bomber, LL344-P.
644 Sqn 38 Group RAF: F/O Clapperton, F/O Roberts, F/Sgt

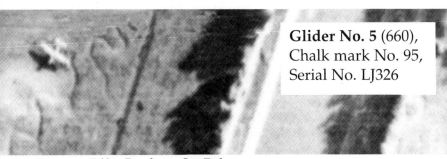

Glider No. 5 (660),
Chalk mark No. 95,
Serial No. LJ326

Burness, F/Sgt Bareham, Sgt Rolt.

Glider Pilot Regiment: S/Sgt Pearson, S/Sgt Guthrie.
No. 23 Pl D Coy 2 Oxf Bucks: Lt Sweeney (Platoon

Commander), Sgt Gooch, Cpl Howard, Cpl Jennings, Cpl Murton, L/Cpl Porter, L/Cpl Stacey, Pte Allen, Pte Bleach, Pte Bowden, Pte Bright, Pte Buller, Pte Clark 46, Pte Galbraith, Pte Jackson 59, Pte Read, Pte Roach, Pte Roberts, Pte Tibbett, Pte Willcocks, Pte Wixen, Pte Wood.

7 Para: Lt Macdonald (Liaison Officer).

No. 2 Pl 249 Fd Coy RE: Cpl Straw, Spr Bradford, Spr Carter, Spr Field, Spr Wilkinson.

Tug: Halifax bomber, LL406-T.

298 Sqn 38 Group RAF: W/O Bain, F/L Rowell, Sgt Holder, F/S Mansell, Sgt Weeks, Sgt Beusley.

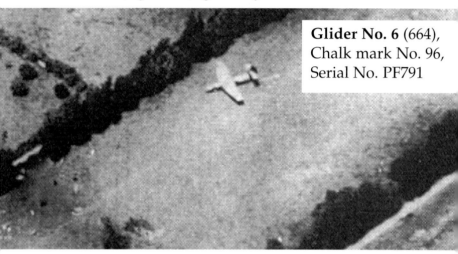

Glider No. 6 (664), Chalk mark No. 96, Serial No. PF791

Glider Pilot Regiment: S/Sgt Howard, S/Sgt Baacke.

No. 17 Pl B Coy 2 Oxf Bucks: Lt Fox (Platoon Commander), Sgt Thornton, Cpl Burns, Cpl Lally, Cpl Reynolds, L/Cpl Loveday, Pte Annetts, Pte Clare, Pte Collett, Pte Hubbert, Pte Lawton, Pte O'Shaughnessy, Pte Peverill, Pte Pope, Pte Rudge, Pte Storr, Pte Summersby, Pte Ward, Pte Whitbread, Pte Whitehouse, Pte Woods, Pte Wyatt.

RAMC: L/Cpl Lawson.

No. 2 Pl 249 Fd Coy RE: Lt Bence, Spr Burns, Spr Larkin C.H., Spr Larkin C.W. Spr Maxted.

Tug: Halifax bomber, LL350-Z.

644 Sqn 38 Group RAF: F/O Archibald, F/S O'Shea, Sgt Hones, F/Sgt Chidley, F/Sgt Brown (RCAF), Sgt Orford.

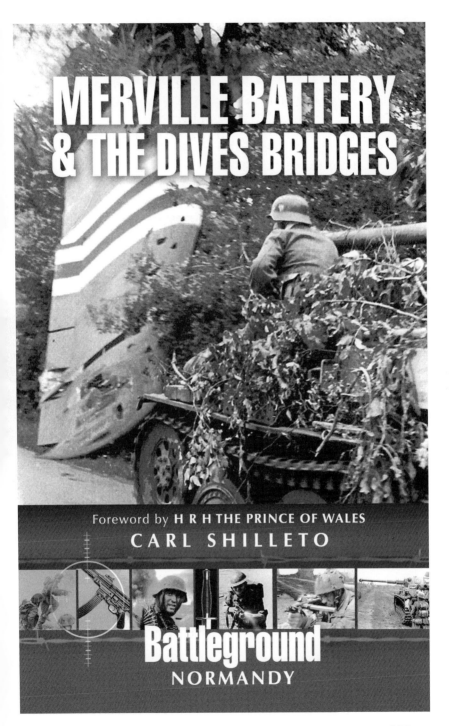

MERVILLE BATTERY
& THE DIVES BRIDGES

Foreword by **H R H THE PRINCE OF WALES**
CARL SHILLETO

Battleground
NORMANDY

MERVILLE BATTERY
& THE DIVES BRIDGES
Carl Shilleto

*Foreword **HRH The Prince of Wales***

This battlefield guide is the companion work to **Pegasus Bridge & Horsa Bridge**. Together, these two books form the fully revised and updated edition of the previous best selling **Battleground Europe Series** book **Pegasus Bridge & Merville Battery.**

This book examines, in great detail, the attack by 9 Para Bn of the British 6th Airborne Division on the German gun emplacement known as the Merville Battery on D-Day, 6 June 1944. The actions of 8 Para, 12 Para, Canadian 1 Para, attached engineer and support units, and commando raids in this area of Normandy are also told. In particular, the importance of destroying the five bridges, and a drainage culvert, in the Dives valley are explained along with the importance of taking and holding the high ground to the north-east of Caen. These combined actions resulted in the protection and securing of the left flank of the greatest combined military operation in history; Operation OVERLORD.

In addition to explaining how these objectives were achieved, this battlefield guide relates the battles to the area as it is today. The book contains details of the museums, memorials, cemeteries and associated organisations. All of which will unravel the history of the area to the visitor and armchair traveller alike.

To further aid the battlefield tourist, GPS data is also provided for either satellite navigation by vehicle or for viewing on Google Earth.

ISBN: 978-1-84884-519-0

Paperback

184

Postscript

At just after midday on Tuesday 19 April 2011, Flight Lieutenant Henry 'Lacy' Smith, a Royal Australian Air Force pilot of No. 453 Sqaudron RAF, was laid to rest in Ranville Commonwealth War Cemetery.

His aircraft, Spitfire LF 1XB MJ had been shot down by 20mm anti-aircraft fire on Sunday 11 June 1944 while patrolling over the coast east of Ouistreham and area of operations for the 6th Airborne Division. Ditching his aircraft, while trying to make for land, his remains and aircraft subsequently remained submerged, and all but forgotten, in the waters and mud flats of the Orne estuary for over half a century.

In November, 2010, thanks to the efforts of two locals, Brigitte and Fabrice Corbin, the body of Flight Lieutenant Smith, and remains of his Spitfire were recovered. The aircraft wreckage is to be preserved and displayed at the RAAF Museum at Point Cook, Australia. Twenty-seven year old Flight Lieutenant Smith now rests alongside another 2,242 men in Ranville Cemetery who also paid the ultimate price for freedom in the battle for Normandy.